Advanced Lessons in English: For Advanced Grammar Grades, High Schools, Academies, and Ungraded Schools

Mary Frances Hyde

BIBLIOLIFE

ADVANCED LESSONS
IN ENGLISH

FOR

ADVANCED GRAMMAR GRADES, HIGH SCHOOLS,
ACADEMIES, AND UNGRADED SCHOOLS.

BY

MARY F. HYDE,

AUTHOR OF "PRACTICAL LESSONS IN THE USE OF ENGLISH."

———— ∘∘❖∘∘ ————

BOSTON, U.S.A.:
D. C. HEATH & CO., PUBLISHERS.
1893.

PREFACE.

THIS book is designed for advanced classes in grammar schools, or for pupils in high schools, academies, or ungraded schools, who desire a brief, practical, progressive course in English grammar. It is specially adapted to the needs of pupils who have completed the second book in the author's series entitled, "Practical Lessons in the Use of English," but it can be used independently of that work or of that series.

The aim of the work is not to teach the greatest possible number of facts about the English language, but to give the pupil a mastery of the leading grammatical principles as a means toward the right understanding and correct use of English.

The thorough training in essential principles which the pupil must receive from the use of this book will furnish him the best possible preparation for higher English studies or for the study of other languages.

The work does not consist of a mere statement of definitions and rules. Every principle is presented through the study of examples, by which means the pupil's knowledge of grammatical facts is based upon his own observation.

Examples illustrating the points to be presented precede the general statements of principles, that the pupil may be led from the observation of particular facts to general conclusions. The sentences for study have been selected with great care from the works of our best writers, and, where space would admit, the names of the authors have been given. This method of studying English trains the pupil to look to the usage of the best writers and speakers for the laws of language, and forms in him the habit of thoughtful reading.

The book contains not only sentences for the development of the various topics, but also a storehouse of examples illustrating different grammatical points. These examples can be used not only in connection with the lessons in which they appear, but with other lessons as well. The skillful teacher will make use of these sentences for supplementary exercises adapted to the special needs of the class.

The book is divided into four parts. Part First treats of "KINDS OF WORDS — the Parts of Speech"; Part Second, of "CLASSES AND FORMS OF WORDS — Subdivision of the Parts of Speech, and Inflection"; Part Third, of "RELATIONS OF WORDS — Syntax"; and Part Fourth, of the "STRUCTURE AND ANALYSIS OF SENTENCES."

My thanks are returned to all who have given me the benefit of their suggestions during the preparation of this work. I feel specially indebted to Professor Edward S. Joynes of the University of South Carolina, and to Professor Thomas R. Price of Columbia College, for invaluable criticisms during the progress of the work through the press.

M. F. H

CONTENTS.

PART FIRST.

KINDS OF WORDS — THE PARTS OF SPEECH.

LESSON I.

THE SENTENCE.

How many thoughts are expressed in the following sentences? —

1. The village master taught his little school.
2. Keep thy tongue from evil.
3. Who planted this old apple-tree?
4. How are the mighty fallen!

The expression of a complete thought in words is called **a sentence.**

State the office or use of each sentence above — tell which sentence states or declares something, which expresses a command, etc.

A sentence that states or declares something is called a **declarative sentence.**

A sentence that expresses a command or an entreaty is called an **imperative sentence.**

A sentence that asks a question is called an **interrogative sentence.**

A sentence that expresses sudden or strong feeling is called an **exclamatory sentence.**

EXERCISE I.

State the office of each of the following sentences, and tell the kind of sentence : —

1. The last ray of sunshine departed.
2. Every stranger finds a ready chair.
3. How fleet is a glance of the mind!
4. The boat was crowded with passengers.
5. Dark clouds began to rise in the west.
6. The troops were concealed by a thick wood.
7. What an admirable piece of work this is!
8. Apply thine heart to understanding.
9. How many entered the room?
10. Consider the lilies of the field.
11. What was the result?
12. I sat beside the glowing grate.

EXERCISE II.

1. *Write three declarative sentences.*
2. *Write three imperative sentences.*
3. *Write three interrogative sentences.*
4. *Write three exclamatory sentences.*

LESSON II.

SUBJECT AND PREDICATE.

Tell what is spoken of in each of the following sentences, and what is said about the thing spoken of : —

1. Time flies swiftly.
2. A rolling stone gathers no moss.
3. The breaking waves dashed high.

The part of a sentence that shows what is spoken of is called the **subject**.

The part of a sentence that tells something about the thing spoken of is called the **predicate**.

To find the subject and the predicate, answer the questions: (1) What is this sentence about? (2) What is said or asked about it?

The subject and the predicate may each be expressed by a single word, or by several words; as, —

Bells | ring.

A merciful man | considers his beast.

The subject of a declarative sentence is usually placed before the predicate; as, —

The well-curb had a Chinese roof.

But sometimes, especially in poetry, the subject is placed after the predicate; as, —

Up springs *the lark.*

Sweet is *the breath of morn.*

EXERCISE I.

Name the subject and the predicate in each of the following sentences : —

1. The whole island was covered with wood.
2. The first spring wild-flowers yield no honey.
3. The old oaken bucket hangs in the well.

4. Blessed are the pure in heart.

5. The first dragon-fly of the season is always a happy discovery.

6. These prairies glow with flowers.

7. The copper of Cyprus was in demand in most places of the ancient world.

8. All bloodless lay the untrodden snow.

9. For three nights they floated down the stream.

10. Language is the highest mode of expression.

The subject of an imperative sentence is *thou, ye,* or *you.* It is generally not expressed; as, —

Come into the garden.

When the subject is expressed, it is placed after the verb; as, —

Praise *ye* the Lord.

EXERCISE II.

Copy the following sentences, supplying the subjects which are understood and enclosing them in brackets : —

1. Listen to this account of the fire.
2. Fling wide the generous grain.
3. Throw part of the cargo overboard.
4. Speak gently to the erring.
5. Cleanse thou me from secret faults.
6. Rejoice in the prosperity of others.
7. Be not weary in well-doing.
8. Follow the directions carefully.

Example. — Listen [*you*] to this account of the fire.

State the kind of sentence, and name the subject and the predicate in each of the following sentences : —

1. When will the matter be settled?
2. Here we are at last!
3. What peaceful hours I once enjoyed!
4. Where does he live?
5. Where are a grasshopper's ears?
6. How lightly past hardship sits upon us!
7. What real service to others did you render yesterday?
8. How strange everything looks in this light!
9. Do your friends know this?
10. How blessings brighten as they take their flight!

Write three examples each of a declarative, an imperative, an interrogative, and an exclamatory sentence, and name the subject and the predicate in each sentence.

LESSON III.

NOUNS.

Mention the words in the following sentences that are used as names, and tell what each is the name of : —

ı. America has furnished to the world the character of Washington.

2 The chair stood by the window.

3. The maples redden in the sun.

Mention a word used as the name of a person; the name of a place; the name of a thing that you can see, feel, hear, smell, or touch; the name of a thing that you can think of but cannot perceive by the senses; the name of a quality of a person or thing; the name of an action.

A word used as a name is called a **noun**.

EXERCISE I.

Mention the nouns in the following sentences, and tell what kind of thing each names: —

1.   He goes on Sunday to the church
        And sits among his boys.

2. Then Evangeline lighted the brazen lamp on the table.

3. A large island covered with palms divides the Nile into two branches.

4. His door was always open to the wayfarer.

5. Hear me with patience.

6. The time of the singing of birds is come.

7. He came early in the spring to the settlement of New Plymouth.

8.   The breeze comes whispering in our ear,
        That dandelions are blossoming near,
        That maize has sprouted, that streams are flowing,
        That the river is bluer than the sky,

That the robin is plastering his house hard by;
And if the breeze kept the good news back,
For other couriers we should not lack. — LOWELL.

EXERCISE II.

I. *Write sentences containing* —

1. The name of a person.
2. The name of a place.
3. The name of a public building.
4. The name of a material used in building houses.
5. The name of an article of dress.
6. The name of a part of the human body.
7. The name of a feeling.
8. The name of an action.

II. *Name the subject and the predicate in each of the sentences written.*

LESSON IV.

PRONOUNS.

For what nouns are the italicized words used in the following sentences? —

1. Henry paused, when *he* reached the door.
2. The travellers looked surprised, when *they* heard the story.

3. *I* met a little cottage girl,
She was eight years old, *she* said.

A word used for a noun is called a **pronoun**. By the use of the pronoun, we can avoid the mention or repetition of the noun for which it stands. The use of the pronoun *I* saves the mention of the speaker's name; the pronoun *it* refers to something that has been previously mentioned, etc.

EXERCISE I.

Mention the pronouns in the following sentences, and state for what each is used: —

1. Train up a child in the way he should go.

2. Nearly all the night insects are comparatively noiseless in their flight.

3. The books remain where you left them.

4. When I turned again to look for the bird, I could not see it.

5. Trust men and they will be true to you; treat them greatly and they will show themselves great.

6. Not a soldier discharged his farewell shot
O'er the grave where our hero we buried.

7. She folded her arms beneath her cloak.

8. As the route of the friends lay in the same direction, they agreed to perform the rest of their journey together.

9. So intent were the servants upon their sports, that we had to ring repeatedly before we could make ourselves heard.

10. A belted kingfisher suddenly appeared in the air just in front of me, where he hovered for a moment as if doubtful whether to fly over us and go up the river or to turn about and retreat before us.

EXERCISE II.

Write sentences containing pronouns used for—

1. The name of the speaker.
2. The name of a person spoken to.
3. The name of a person spoken of.
4. The names of two or more persons spoken of.
5. The names of the speaker and others.
6. The name of a thing that has been previously mentioned.
7. The names of two or more things that have been previously mentioned.

LESSON V.

ADJECTIVES.

Find the words in the following sentences that are used with nouns, to describe or point out the things named : —

1. A small boat approached the shore.
2. The plant had glossy leaves.
3. Two doves circled in the air.
4. This package was not opened.

The word *small* limits the application of the noun *boat* to a particular kind of boat. The word *the* limits the application of the noun *plant* to a particular plant.

A word that describes or limits the meaning of another word is said to modify that word ; as, *clear* water ; *the* boy.

A word used to modify a noun or a pronoun is called an **adjective.**

Mention five adjectives that are used with nouns, to express the kind or quality of the objects named; five adjectives that denote quantity or number; three adjectives that point out the thing spoken of.

EXERCISE I.

Name the adjectives in the following sentences, and state the use of each:—

1. Two ships were anchored in the bay.
2. Blue were her eyes as the fairy flax.
3. A wise son maketh a glad father.
4. Brave hearts were ready for bold deeds.
5. These people are honest, kind-hearted, and industrious.
6. The statue is nearly seven feet in height.
7. The wax candles were now lighted, and showed a handsome room, well provided with rich furniture.
8. The doe was a beauty, with slender limbs, not too heavy flanks, round body, and aristocratic head, with small ears, and luminous, intelligent, affectionate eyes.—C. D. WARNER.

9.   His withered cheek and tresses gray,
       Seemed to have known a better day.

Example.—The adjectives in the first sentence are *two* and *the*. *Two* shows how many ships were anchored in the bay, and *the* points out a particular bay.

EXERCISE II.

Write five sentences containing adjectives used to show —

1. What kind of thing is meant.
2. How many things are meant.
3. How much of a quantity is mentioned.
4. Which thing is spoken of.

LESSON VI.

VERBS.

Point out the words in the following sentences, that tell or assert something of the thing named : —

    1. Birds sing.
    2. The wind blows.
    3. He is a soldier.

A word that asserts is called a **verb**; as, The sun *rose*.

The word that denotes the person or thing about which the assertion is made is called the **subject** * of the verb; as, The *sun* rose.

EXERCISE I.

Mention the verbs in the following sentences, and state what each tells : —

1. The curfew tolls the knell of parting day.
2. He springs from his hammock, he flies to the deck.
3. The pigeons fly in great clouds from village to village.
4. The kettle sings, the cat in chorus purrs.
5. They robbed the wild bees of their honey, and chased the deer over the hills.
6. The horses neighed, and the oxen lowed.
7. She pointed to the web of beautifully woven cloth in the loom.
8. A fire blazed brightly on the hearth.
9. The shadows dance upon the wall.

* See foot-note on page 76

10.   When breezes are soft and skies are fair,
        I steal an hour from study and care.

11. Thus the night passed. The moon went down; the stars grew pale; the cold day broke; the sun rose.

EXERCISE II.

Write sentences containing the following words used (1) *as nouns,* (2) *as verbs :* —

bark,	walk,	fear,	sail,	salt,
rock,	look,	dream,	fire,	hope.

EXERCISE III.

Write sentences containing the following words used as the subjects of verbs. Underline the verbs : —

moon,	iron,	soldier,	singer,	wind,
courage,	grocer,	river,	organ,	bell.

LESSON VII.

ADVERBS.

Point out the words in the following sentences that show *how, when,* or *where* actions were performed : —

1. The boat moves slowly.
2. He always spoke the truth.
3. The child stood here.

Mention the verb in each sentence, and tell what word modifies its meaning.

A word that modifies the meaning of a verb is called an **adverb**.

Sometimes an adverb is used to modify the meaning of an adjective ; as, —

 1. It is a *very* cold day.
 2. The sleeve is *too* short.

Sometimes an adverb is used to modify the meaning of another adverb ; as, —

 1. *How* gently the rain falls!
 2. Do not walk so fast.

An **adverb** is a word that modifies the meaning of a verb, an adjective, or another adverb.

EXERCISE I.

Mention the adverbs in the following sentences, and tell what each modifies : —

 1. She passed hastily down the street.
 2. She turned, and looked back.
 3. How hard a lesson it is to wait!
 4. How silently the snow falls!
 5. The common wild birds of the woods were everywhere.
 6. Faster and faster we sped.
 7. The shower soon passed.
 8. The statement is perfectly correct.

 9. But we steadfastly gazed on the face that was dead,
  And we bitterly thought of the morrow. — WOLFE.

 10. Now fades the glimmering landscape on the sight.
—GRAY.

1. *Write five sentences containing adverbs modifying verbs.*
2. *Write three sentences containing adverbs modifying adjectives.*
3. *Write two sentences containing adverbs modifying adverbs.*

LESSON VIII.

PREPOSITIONS.

Point out the words in the following sentences that show the relation of a noun or pronoun to some other word : —

1. They sailed up the river.
2. No one spoke to him.
3. The clock in the steeple struck three.
4. She is fond of music.

A word used with a noun or pronoun to show its relation to some other word in the sentence is called a **preposition**; as, —

The leaves fell *to* the ground.

The noun or pronoun before which the preposition is placed is called its **object**; as, —

The boat is on the *shore.*

The preposition usually joins a noun or pronoun to a verb, an adjective, or another noun ; as, —

1. He *lived* [verb] *by* the *river*.
2. They are *ready* [adjective] *for battle*.
3. It is a *book* [noun] *of selections*.

EXERCISE I.

Mention the prepositions in the following sentences, tell between what words each shows a relation, and name its object :—

1. A fair little girl sat under a tree.
2. The dining-table stood in the centre of the room.
3. The boy was pleased at the prospect of taking a long journey.
4. At midnight I was aroused by the tramp of horses' hoofs in the yard.
5. The habits of our American cuckoo are extremely interesting.
6. Into the street the Piper stept.
7. They were eager for the contest.

8.   Every day the starving poor
     Crowded around Bishop Hatto's door. — Southey.

9. Like the leaves of the forest, when summer is green,
That host with their banners at sunset were seen.

10.   I see the lights of the village
     Gleam through the rain and the mist.

EXERCISE II.

1. *Write five sentences, each containing a preposition expressing a relation between a verb and a noun or a pronoun.*

2. Write five sentences, each containing a preposition expressing a relation between two nouns.

3. Write three sentences, each containing a preposition expressing a relation between an adjective and a noun.

LESSON IX.

CONJUNCTIONS.

Point out the words in the following examples, that connect sentences or similar parts of the same sentence : —

1. The walls are high, and the shores are steep.
2. They came, but they did not stay.
3. Slowly and sadly we laid him down.
4.   We have been friends together,
        In sunshine and in shade.

A word that connects sentences or similar parts of the same sentence is called a **conjunction**.

EXERCISE I.

Point out the conjunctions in the following sentences, and tell what each connects : —

1. The floods came, and the winds blew.
2. Freely we serve, because we freely love.
3. He reached the well, but nobody was there.
4. The ploughman homeward plods his weary way,
    And leaves the world to darkness and to me. —GRAY.

5. She must weep, or she will die. — TENNYSON.

6. The very flames danced and capered in the polished grate.

7. Sink or swim, live or die, survive or perish, I give my heart and my hand to this vote. — DANIEL WEBSTER.

8. Three years she grew in sun and shower. — WORDSWORTH.

9.   The waves beside them danced; but they
        Outdid the sparkling waves in glee. — WORDSWORTH.

10. Blessed are the merciful, for they shall obtain mercy. — BIBLE.

EXERCISE II.

Write sentences containing conjunctions connecting —

1. Two sentences.
2. Two nouns.
3. Two adjectives.
4. Two verbs.
5. Two adverbs.

——◦◦◦——

LESSON X.

INTERJECTIONS.

What words in the following sentences form no part of either subject or predicate ? —

1. Alas! we have delayed too long.
2. Hark! was that a knock?
3. Hurrah! the foes are moving.

What feeling is expressed by the use of the word *alas?* By the word *hark?* By the word *hurrah?*

A word used to indicate some sudden feeling is called an **interjection.**

Interjections may express —

    1. Joy; as, *hurrah! huzzah!*

    2. Pain or suffering; as, *ah! oh! alas!*

    3. Surprise; as, *ha! lo! what!*

    4. Disapproval; as, *fie! fudge!*

    5. A call for attention; as, *ho! hey! hark!*

                 Etc., etc.

EXERCISE I.

Mention the interjections in the following sentences, and tell what each expresses: —

    1. Alas! I am undone.

    2. Away! we must not linger.

    3. Hush! it is the dead of night.

    4. Halloo! who stands guard here?

    5. Ah! whence is that flame which now glares on his eye?

    6. Oh! how many broken bonds of affection were here!

    7. But hush! hark! a deep sound strikes like a rising knell.

    8. Ha! feel ye not your fingers thrill?

    9. Alas! they all are in their graves.

    10. Oh! the boat is safe enough.

    11. O look! the sun begins to rise.

12.   And lo! from the assembled crowd
       There rose a shout, prolonged and loud.

EXERCISE II.

Write ten sentences, each containing one of the following interjections : —

hark!	whew!	ho!	hurrah!	hush!
fy!	pshaw!	alas!	ah!	fudge!

LESSON XI.

PARTS OF SPEECH.

REVIEW EXERCISE.

Mention some of the different parts performed by words in a sentence.

What do we call a word that is used as a name ?   A word used instead of a noun ?   A word that asserts ?

How many classes of words are used as modifiers ?   What are these classes called ?   How does the adjective differ from the adverb?

How many kinds of connecting words are there ?   What are they called?   In what way are prepositions and conjunctions alike?   How do they differ?

Mention a class of words not connected with the other words in a sentence.

How many kinds of words have been considered ?

The different classes of words used in sentences are called **parts of speech.**   They are so named from the different *parts* they perform in the sentence.

SUMMARY OF THE PARTS OF SPEECH.

1. **A** noun is a word used as a name.

2. **A** pronoun is a word used for a noun.

3. **An** adjective is a word used to modify a noun or a pronoun.

4. **A** verb is a word that asserts.

5. **An** adverb is a word that modifies a verb, an adjective, or another adverb.

6. **A** preposition is a word placed before a noun or pronoun, to show its relation to some other word in the sentence.

7. **A** conjunction is a word that connects sentences or similar parts of the same sentence.

8. **An** interjection is a word used to indicate some sudden feeling.

EXERCISE I.

Tell whether the italicized words in the following sentences are adverbs or prepositions, giving reasons in each case: —

1. Is your employer *within?*
2. The work will be done *within* a week.
3. It rolled *down* the hill.
4. Slowly and sadly we laid him *down.*
5. A voice replied far *up* the height.
6. Lift *up* thine eyes unto the hills.
7. They passed *by.*
8. He sat *by* the well.
9. Your hat is *behind* the door.
10. Do not lag *behind.*

11. A beautiful picture hung *above* the altar.
12. The eagle soars *above*.
13. None *but* the brave deserve the fair.
14. Man wants *but* little here below.

EXERCISE II.

Show which of the words in Italics in the following sentences are prepositions and which are conjunctions: —

1. They came, *but* they did not remain.
2. He cares for nothing *but* money.
3. All the family were present, *except* one son.
4. *Except* ye repent, ye shall all likewise perish.
5. I have not heard from them *since* yesterday.
6. *Since* you are here, you might remain.
7. The children ran *after* the procession.
8. He came *after* the exercises had closed.
9. The building will be completed *before* the leaves fall.
10. It stands *before* the fireplace.
11. Stay here *until* I come.
12. They will remain abroad *until* November
13. He died *for* his country.
14. Our bugles sang truce; *for* the night-cloud had lowered.

EXERCISE III.

Distinguish between the offices of the italicized words in each of the following examples: —

1. Then rushed the steed to *battle* driven. The troops appeared in *battle* array.

2. *Farewell!* a long *farewell*, to all my greatness.   Not a soldier discharged his *farewell* shot.

3. It was over in one *second.*   Omit the *second* stanza. I *second* the motion.

4. He is as *good* as he is strong.   Who will show us any *good?*

5. They visited a *far* country.   *Far* flashed the red artillery.

6. This is the *best* answer that was given.

> He prayeth *best* who loveth *best*
> All things both great and small.

7. The horse is a *fast* walker.   The child is *fast* asleep. When ye *fast*, be not, as the hypocrites, of a sad countenance.   The shades of night were falling *fast.*

8. He is *still* here.   Now came *still* evening on.   There is a good fire, *still* the room is cold.

EXERCISE IV.

State the office of each italicized word in the following sentences, and tell what part of speech it is : —

1. His *to-days* are never *yesterdays.*
2. The lion shall lie *down* with the lamb.
3. As I looked *up*, I saw the boat *before* me.
4. There is a *calm* for those who weep.
5. The laborer is worthy of his *hire.*
6. The good south wind still blew *behind.*
7. It is not finished *yet.*
8.   Swiftly, swiftly sailed the ship:
    Yet she sailed softly too.

9. *Ere* I go, you must consent.

10. Think, *before* you speak.

11. *Still* waters run deep.

12. We look *before* and *after*.

13. The *down* train is late.

14. He had experienced many *ups* and *downs* in life.

15. *Up* went the steps, *bang* went the door, *round* whirled the wheels, and *off* they rattled.

16. We talked *about* the trees.

17.   On *right*, on *left*, *above*, *below*,
       Sprung *up* at once the lurking foe.

18. The *very* village was altered.

19. Arise, take *up* thy bed, and go *unto* thy house.

EXERCISE V.

1. *Write sentences containing the following words used as nouns :* —

to-morrow,   fear,   paper,   ring,   America.

2. *Write sentences containing the following words used as verbs :* —

stand,   fear,   paper,   ring,   water.

3. *Write sentences containing the following words used as adverbs :* —

to-morrow,   after,   before,   since,   over.

4. *Write sentences containing the following words used as prepositions :* —

till,   before,   after,   over,   for.

5. *Write sentences containing the following words used as conjunctions:* —

till,   before,   after,   since,   for.

To the Teacher. — Give additional exercises, if they are needed, to impress the fact, that it is not the form of a word, but the part it performs in a sentence, that determines what *part of speech* the word is.

PART SECOND.

CLASSES AND FORMS OF WORDS — SUBDIVISIONS OF THE PARTS OF SPEECH, AND INFLECTION.

LESSON XII.

CLASSES OF NOUNS.

PROPER AND COMMON NOUNS.

Point out in the following sentences (1) the nouns that name special persons or things, (2) the nouns that apply to every one of a class of persons or things : —

1. In the early twilight of Thanksgiving Eve came Laurence, and Clara, and Charley, and little Alice, hand in hand, and stood in a semicircle round Grandfather's chair. — HAWTHORNE.

2. There groups of merry children played.

3. The robin and the wren are flown. — BRYANT.

A name that belongs to an individual person or thing is called a **proper noun**; as, *Clarence, New York, Thursday, Lake George.*

Proper nouns and words derived from them should begin with capital letters. When a proper noun is made

up of two or more words, each word should generally begin with a capital letter.

A name that applies to every one of a class of persons or things is called a **common noun** ; as, *boy, city, day, lake.*

EXERCISE I.

Write sentences containing —

1. The name of a class of animals.
2. The name of a class of flowers.
3. The name of a class of buildings.
4. The name of a special building.
5. The name of a special city.
6. The name of a special river.
7. The name of an individual soldier.
8. The name of an individual poet.
9. The name of a special battle.
10. The name of a special book.

Collective Nouns.

Point out the nouns in the following sentences that name collections of persons or things, and tell of what each collection is composed : —

1. The speaker was afraid to face the audience.
2. The Assembly adjourned at twelve o'clock.
3. The lowing herd winds slowly o'er the lea. — GRAY.
4. There is no flock, however watched and tended,
   But one dead lamb is there. — LONGFELLOW.

5. Are fleets and armies necessary to a work of love and reconciliation? — PATRICK HENRY.

A noun which in the singular names a collection of persons or things is called a **collective noun**; as, *family, jury, swarm.*

EXERCISE II.

Write sentences containing words used to name a collection of —

ships,	soldiers,	sailors,	wolves,	sheep,
bees,	thieves,	buffaloes,	fish,	chickens.

Abstract Nouns.

Mention each word in the following examples that names the quality or condition of a person or thing; as, —

The length of a river.
The bravery of the soldier.
The growth of the plant.

A noun that names a quality, action, or condition of a person or thing, apart from the person or thing itself, is called an **abstract noun**; as, *goodness, happiness.*

An abstract noun that names an action is sometimes called a **verbal noun**; as, *walking, singing.*

Abstract nouns are formed —

1. From adjectives; as, *brightness* from *bright; honesty* from *honest; patience* from *patient.*

2. From verbs; as, *belief* from *believe; singing* from *sing.*

3. From nouns; as, *childhood* from *child; knavery* from *knave.*

Mention each noun in the following sentences, and state the class to which it belongs : —

1. The child's illness is of an alarming nature.
2. Wisdom is better than strength.
3. He has repented of his folly.
4. The time of the singing of birds is come.
5. His writing was illegible.
6. Charity covereth a multitude of sins.
7. How poor are they that have not patience!
8. How little they knew of the depth, and the strength, and the intenseness of that feeling of resistance to illegal acts of power, which possessed the whole American people!

EXERCISE III.

Write the following words in a column, and opposite each place the corresponding abstract noun.

industrious,	weak,	bright,	warm,	honest,
temperate,	walk,	courageous,	true,	wise,
sweet,	judge,	beautiful,	just,	innocent,
proud,	conceal,	deceive,	high,	dull,
long,	please,	learn,	hard,	pure.

———•••———

LESSON XIII.

NUMBER.

1. Tell how many forms each noun in the following examples has, and whether each form denotes one or more : —

| book, | watch, | fox, | lasso, | potato, |
| books, | watches, | foxes, | lassos, | potatoes. |

The form of a word used in speaking of one thing is called **singular**; the form used in speaking of more than one thing is called **plural**.

When a noun denotes one thing, it is said to be in the **singular number**.

When a noun denotes more than one thing it is said to be in the **plural number**.

Most nouns form the plural by adding *s* to the singular; as, *bird, birds; river, rivers.*

When the singular ends in a sound that does not unite easily with the sound of *s*, some nouns add *es* to the singular, to form the plural; as, *loss, losses; match, matches; thrush, thrushes; tax, taxes.*

Most nouns ending in *o* add *s* to the singular, to form the plural; as, —

| piano, | solo, | folio, | cameo, | canto, |
| portfolio, | octavo, • | quarto, | tyro, | halo. |

Some nouns ending in *o* take *es* in the plural; as, —

| hero, | negro, | cargo, | torpedo, | echo, |
| tomato, | tornado, | potato, | mulatto, | veto. |

2. Mention the ending of the singular nouns in the following examples, and tell how their plurals are formed : —

| city, | story, | day, | chimney, |
| cities, | stories, | days, | chimneys. |

Nouns ending in *y* preceded by a vowel, add *s* to the singular, to form the plural; as, *boy, boys; chimney, chimneys.*

Nouns ending in *y* preceded by a consonant, change *y* to *ies,* to form the plural; as, *city, cities; lily, lilies.*

3. How are the singular nouns in the following examples changed to make each mean more than one? —

proof,	gulf,	fife,
proofs,	gulfs	fifes.

Most nouns ending in *f* or *fe* form the plural by adding *s* to the singular; as, *roof, roofs; safe, safes.*

The following nouns change *f* or *fe* to *ves,* to form the plural: —

leaf,	shelf,	wolf,	loaf,	knife,
half,	beef,	thief,	calf,	life.
wife,	sheaf,	elf,	self,	wharf (or add *s*).

EXERCISE I.

Write the following words in columns, and opposite each word write its plural form: —

path,	gift,	fable,	tree,	gulf,
safe,	truth,	sign,	fife,	valley,
roof,	cliff,	hero,	tornado,	chimney,
muff,	solo,	potato,	torpedo,	piano,
wreath,	alley,	moth,	chief,	handkerchief.

EXERCISE II.

Write sentences containing the plurals of the following nouns: —

body,	kidney,	berry,	jury,	alley,
gallery,	essay,	ferry,	journey,	pulley,
copy,	dairy,	lily,	donkey,	poppy,
daisy,	fly,	city,	pony,	duty.

EXERCISE III.

Make a list of ten nouns, ending in f or fe, that form their plurals by the addition of s, and a list of ten other nouns that form their plurals in ves.

———◦◦◦———

LESSON XIV.

NUMBER.— *Continued.*

1. Mention the plurals below, and tell how they are formed : —

man,	foot,	mouse,	ox,	child,
men,	feet,	mice,	oxen,	children.

Some nouns form the plural by changing the vowel of the singular; as, *man, men; goose, geese; tooth, teeth; foot, feet; mouse, mice* (also changes *s* to *c*).

In a few nouns the plural ends in en; as, *ox, oxen; child, children; brother, brethren.*

2. Give the number of each italicized noun in the following examples, and note its form : —

1. A *deer* came to the shore of the lake.
2. *Deer* have their established runways.

3. A *sheep* before her shearers is dumb.

4. All we like *sheep* have gone astray.

Some nouns have the same form in both numbers; as, *sheep, deer, trout, cannon.*

Some nouns have no singular; as, *ashes, scissors, tongs, trousers.*

Some nouns have two plural forms differing in meaning; as, —

brother, brothers (by blood), *brethren* (by association).
fish, fishes (taken separately), *fish* (taken collectively).
genius, geniuses (men of genius), *genii* (spirits).
index, indexes (of books), *indices* (signs in algebra).
pea, peas (taken separately), *pease* (taken collectively).
penny, pennies (taken separately), *pence* (taken collectively).

EXERCISE I.

Write sentences containing the plurals of the following nouns, and tell how each plural is formed: —

woman,	foot,	cannon,	shad,	deer,
tooth,	ox,	mouse,	fish,	genius,
sheaf,	enemy,	buoy,	crutch,	reef,
wharf,	colloquy,	envoy,	life,	fife.

EXERCISE II.

Make a list of the following nouns, and opposite each write its singular: —

genii,	peas,	pence,	brethren,	indices,
beeves,	brothers,	fishes,	pease,	pennies,
lives,	indexes,	women,	sheaves,	halves.

LESSON XV.

NUMBER. — *Continued.*

1. Tell how each plural form below is made from the singular : —

spoonful,	brother-in-law,	man-servant,
spoonfuls,	brothers-in-law,	men-servants.

Some compound nouns form the plural like single words, others make the principal word plural, and a few change both words ; as, *cupful, cupfuls ; mother-in-law, mothers-in-law ; woman-servant, women-servants.*

EXERCISE I.

Write the singulars of the following nouns, and tell how the plurals are formed : —

grandfathers,	maid-servants,	merchantmen,
eyelashes,	attorneys-at-law,	greenhouses,
tooth-brushes,	countrymen,	forget-me-nots,
fathers-in-law,	commanders-in-chief,	women-servants,
sisters-in-law,	men-of-war,	knights-templars.

2. **When a title is prefixed to a proper name, the compound may be made plural by changing either the title or the name ; as, the *Misses* Brown or the Miss *Browns*.**

The title is made plural when it is used with two or more names ; as, *Messrs.* Stone and Wood.

Letters, figures, and signs add the apostrophe (') and *s*, to form the plural ; as, Dot the *i's ;* Cancel the *5's ;* Write the +'s on a straight line.

Many nouns taken from foreign languages retain their original plurals. The following are a few of the most common : —

SINGULAR.	PLURAL.	SINGULAR.	PLURAL.
formula,	formulæ,	larva,	larvæ,
alumnus,	alumni,	radius,	radii,
animalculum,	animalcula,	genius,	genii,
erratum,	errata,	memorandum,	memoranda,
stratum,	strata,	vertex,	vertices,
index,	indices,	axis,	axes,
analysis,	analyses,	basis,	bases,
crisis,	crises,	phenomenon,	phenomena,
beau,	beaux,	bandit,	banditti,
cherub,	cherubim,	seraph,	seraphim.

Some foreign words which are in common use form the plural in the usual way, often with a difference of meaning; as, *formulas, indexes, geniuses.*

EXERCISE II.

Make a list of the foregoing singular nouns from foreign languages, and opposite each write from memory its plural.

LESSON XVI.

GENDER

Which words in the following list denote males? Which denote females? —

man,	father,	host,	man-servant,
woman,	mother,	hostess,	maid-servant.

A noun that denotes a male is said to be of the **masculine gender**; as, *man, heir*.

A noun that denotes a female is said to be of the **feminine gender**; as, *woman, heiress*.

A noun that may denote either a male or a female is said to be of the **common gender**; as, *parent, friend, robin*.

A noun that denotes a thing neither male nor female is said to be of the **neuter gender**; as, *book, sky, joy*.

The gender of nouns is distinguished in three ways: —

1. **By different words**; as, —

MASCULINE.	FEMININE.	MASCULINE.	FEMININE.
bachelor,	maid,	husband,	wife,
boy,	girl,	king,	queen,
brother,	sister,	monk,	nun,
buck,	doe,	lord,	lady,
cock,	hen,	nephew,	niece,
drake,	duck,	papa,	mamma,
earl,	countess,	ram,	ewe,
father,	mother,	sir,	madam,
gander,	goose,	son,	daughter,
gentleman,	lady,	stag,	hind,
hart,	roe,	uncle,	aunt,
horse,	mare,	wizard,	witch.

2. **By different endings.** The chief feminine ending is **ess**, but other endings appear in some words; as, —

MASCULINE.	FEMININE.	MASCULINE.	FEMININE.
baron,	baroness,	benefactor,	benefactress,
count,	countess,	emperor,	empress,

MASCULINE.	FEMININE.	MASCULINE.	FEMININE.
heir,	heiress,	duke,	duchess,
host,	hostess,	master,	mistress,
Jew,	Jewess,	tiger,	tigress,
lion,	lioness,	administrator,	administratrix,
patron,	patroness,	executor,	executrix,
prince,	princess,	hero,	heroine,
abbot,	abbess,	Paul,	Pauline,
governor,	governess,	czar,	czarina,
negro,	negress,	Augustus,	Augusta,
actor,	actress,	sultan,	sultana.

3. **By prefixing words indicating the sex; as,—**

MASCULINE.	FEMININE.
man-servant,	maid-servant,
men-singers,	women-singers,
he-goat,	she-goat.

EXERCISE I.

Make a list of all the masculine nouns mentioned in this lesson, and opposite each write from memory the corresponding feminine noun.

EXERCISE II.

Point out the masculine, the feminine, and the neuter nouns in the following sentences, and tell which nouns may denote either males or females:—

1. We learned the ways of the fish, the birds, the bees, the winds, the clouds, the flowers.

2. Night closed in, but still no guest arrived.

3. Leaving the boatmen at the camp, I spent the greater part of the night in the very heart of a jungle.

4. Temperance and labor are the two best physicians of man.

5. Though Grandfather was old and gray-haired, yet his heart leaped with joy whenever little Alice came fluttering, like a butterfly, into the room. — HAWTHORNE.

6. I have had playmates, I have had companions. — CHARLES LAMB.

7. Brethren, the sower's task is done. — BRYANT.

8. I rise, my Lords, to declare my sentiments on this most solemn and serious subject. — BURKE.

9. Little Effie shall 'go with me to-morrow to the green,
   And you'll be there, too, mother, to see me made the
   Queen. — TENNYSON.

10. Brothers, sisters, husbands, wives,
    Followed the Piper for their lives. — ROBERT BROWNING.

11. The lamps shone o'er fair women and brave men.
— BYRON.

12. What would we give to our beloved?
    The hero's heart, to be unmoved,
       The poet's star-tuned harp, to sweep,
    The patriot's voice, to teach and rouse,
    The monarch's crown, to light the brows? —
       He giveth His beloved sleep. — E. B. BROWNING.

LESSON XVII.

CASE.

Mention the subjects of the verbs in the following sentences: —

1. The boy bought a watch.
2. An officer caught the thief.
3. Birds build nests.

What did the boy buy? *Whom* did the officer catch? *What* do birds build? Which words limit the actions expressed by the verbs?

The noun or pronoun that limits the action expressed by a verb is called the **object** of the verb.

State the offices of the italicized words in the following: —

1. We followed the *shepherd's* dog.
2. The *horse's* bridle is broken.

When a word is used to show to whom or to what something belongs, it is said to denote possession.

Find in the following sentences a noun used (1) as the subject of a verb, (2) as the object of a verb, (3) as the object of a preposition, (4) to denote possession: —

1. The boy stood by the door.
2. He heard his father's voice.
3. A wave upset the boat.
4. The traveller walked through the fields.

The relation which a noun or pronoun bears to some other word in the sentence is called **case**.

A noun used as the subject of a verb is said to be in the **nominative case**; as, —

The *bell* rang.

A noun used to show possession is said to be in the **possessive case**; as, —

The *child's* eyes are blue.

A noun used as the object of a verb or of a preposition is said to be in the **objective case**; as, —

1. They launched the *vessel.*
2. He gazed at the *flowers.*

The case of a noun is determined by the relation that it bears to some other word in the sentence. The possessive case of nouns is the only one that has a special form. The common or ordinary form of the noun is used in the other cases.

The alteration in the form of a word to express a change of meaning is called **inflection**. Nouns are inflected to indicate number and case. A noun is said to be **declined** when its number and case forms are regularly arranged; as, —

	NOM. AND OBJ CASE.	POSSESSIVE CASE.
Singular.	boy,	boy's,
Plural.	boys,	boys'.

EXERCISE I.

State the kind, the gender, the number, and the case of the nouns in the following sentences : —

1. This tree stood in the centre of an ancient wood.
2. The waves rush in on every side.
3. Grandfather's chair stood by the fireside.
4. The stranger shook his head mournfully.

5. Birds have wonderfully keen eyes.

6. He shook his head, shouldered the rusty firelock, and with a heart full of trouble and anxiety turned his steps homeward.

7. Dark lightning flashed from Roderick's eye. — SCOTT.

8. When the rock was hid by the surge's swell,
The mariners heard the warning bell. — SOUTHEY.

9. The rude forefathers of the hamlet sleep. — GRAY.

10. They shook the depths of the desert gloom. — HEMANS.

EXERCISE II.

1. *Write five sentences containing nouns in the nominative case.*

2. *Write five sentences containing nouns in the possessive case.*

3. *Write five sentences containing nouns in the objective case.*

LESSON XVIII.

POSSESSIVE FORMS OF NOUNS.

Mention the nouns that are in the possessive case, and tell how the possessive is formed in each example : —

1. She knelt by the lady's side.
2. The ladies' gallery is closed.
3. Men's voices were heard.

Add the apostrophe and *s* ('s) to a singular noun, to form the possessive; as, *boy, boy's ; man, man's.*

The *s* is sometimes omitted in poetry for the sake of the metre; and it is also omitted in a few words where too many hissing sounds would come together; as, for *conscience'* sake; for *righteousness'* sake; for *Jesus'* sake.

Add the apostrophe (') to a plural noun ending in *s*, to form the possessive; as, *boys, boys'; ladies, ladies'.*

Add the apostrophe and *s* ('s) to a plural noun not ending in *s*, to form the possessive; as, *men, men's; children, children's.*

The possessive sign does not always denote possession. It is used to show authorship, origin, kind, etc.; as, *Lowell's* poems; the *sun's* rays; *men's* clothing.

EXERCISE I.

Point out the nouns in these sentences, tell how each is used, and name its case: —

1. The lark's song rang in her ears.

2. The sound of horses' hoofs was heard in the distance.

3. The scene brought to mind an old writer's account of Christmas preparations.

4. The incidents of the Revolution plentifully supplied the barber's customers with topics of conversation.

5. The boy rang the janitor's bell.

6. A burst of laughter came from the servants' hall.

7. I noted but two warblers' nests during the season.

8.   Vainly the fowler's eye
Might mark thy distant flight to do thee wrong.

9. He felt that his little daughter's love was worth a thousand times more than he had gained by the Golden Touch. — HAWTHORNE.

Write in one column the possessive singular forms, and in another column the possessive plural forms of the following words : —

sister,	woman,	boy,	girl,
mother,	wife,	soldier,	son,
bee,	bird,	friend,	teacher,
poet,	child,	man,	judge.

Example. — SINGULAR. **PLURAL.**

sister's,	sisters',
woman's,	women's.

————

LESSON XIX.

POSSESSIVE FORMS. — *Continued.*

Tell how the possessive case is formed in the following compound words and phrases : —

1. The lieutenant-governor's reverie had now come to an end.

2. Bright and Dun's window is filled with flowers.

3. They are reading Graham and Wood's History.

When a name is composed of two or more words, add the possessive sign to the last word only; as, *Marsh and Wood's* store; *Lee and Peabody's* office.

Two connected nouns implying separate possessions must each take the possessive sign; as, *Webster's and Worcester's* dictionaries.

EXERCISE I.

Explain the possessives in the following examples:—

1. In my father's house are many mansions.

2. Hope vanished from Fitz-James's eye. — Scott.

3. This happened after General Washington's departure from Cambridge.

4. Many a young man ransacked the garret, and brought forth his great-grandfather's sword, corroded with rust and stained with the blood of King Philip's War. — Hawthorne.

5. The rest of the house was in the French taste of Charles the Second's time. — Irving.

6. The grocers', butchers', and fruiterers' shops were thronged with customers. — Irving.

7. Hither they came, from the cornfields, from the clearing in the forest, from the blacksmith's forge, from the carpenter's workshop, and from the shoemaker's seat. — Hawthorne.

8. Let all the ends thou aim'st at be thy country's,
Thy God's, and truth's. — Shakespeare.

9. What good woman does not laugh at her husband's or father's jokes and stories time after time? — Thackeray.

10. These are Clan-Alpine's warriors true. — Scott.

EXERCISE II.

1. *Write five sentences containing connected nouns denoting joint possession.*

2. *Write five sentences containing connected nouns denoting separate possession.*

LESSON XX.

POSSESSIVE FORMS. — *Continued.*

Possession is sometimes indicated by the objective case with the preposition **of**; as, The voice *of the speaker*, for the *speaker's* voice.

This form is generally used in speaking of things without life; as, The lid *of the box;* the bank *of the river.*

This form is preferred also in speaking of persons, when the possessive form would be ambiguous or awkward; as, The wife *of one of my brothers.*

When a thing is personified, the possessive sign is generally used, particularly by the poets; as, —

> And read their history in a nation's eyes. — GRAY.
>
> In reason's ear they all rejoice. — ADDISON.

Certain words and phrases denoting a period of time take the possessive case also; as, A *day's* journey; a *week's* vacation; six *months'* interest.

EXERCISE I.

Explain fully the case of each noun in the following sentences, and point out the examples in which possession is indicated by the objective case with the preposition of: —

1. I flew to the pleasant fields traversed so oft
   In life's morning march, when my bosom was ·young.
   — CAMPBELL.

2. He has not learned the lesson of life who does not every day surmount a fear. — EMERSON.

3. The trade of America had increased far beyond the speculations of the most sanguine imaginations. — BURKE.

4. The poetry of earth is never dead. —KEATS.

5. Either measure would have cost no more than a day's debate. —BURKE.

6. They came without a moment's delay.

7. She has had two years' experience.

8. He likes neither winter's snow nor summer's heat.

9. The city was taken after a ten years' siege.

10. The chieftain's pride was humbled.

EXERCISE II.

Select from standard writers —

1. Ten sentences in which possession is indicated by the objective case with the preposition of.

2. Ten other sentences in which possession is indicated by the use of the possessive sign.

LESSON XXI.

PARSING NOUNS.

To parse a word, tell —

1. Its classification — name the *part of speech*.

2. Its **form** — give the *inflection*, if any.

3. Its **construction** — show its grammatical *relation* to other words in the sentence.

Parse each noun in the following exercises. Tell —

1. The **kind** of noun.

2. Its **number**.

3. Its gender.

4. Its case.

5. Its construction.

Example. — His *eyes* sparkled with *joy* when he heard *Jason's reply*.

1. *Eyes* is a common noun, plural number, neuter gender, nominative case, subject of the verb *sparkled*.*

2. *Joy* is an abstract noun, singular number, neuter gender, objective case, object of the preposition *with*.

3. *Jason's* is a proper noun, singular number, masculine gender, possessive case, depending upon the noun *reply*.

4. *Reply* is a common noun, singular number, neuter gender, objective case, object of the verb *heard*.

EXERCISE L

1. The lights of the church shone through the door.

2. Nell and her grandfather rose from the ground, and took the track through the wood. — DICKENS.

3. The rude forefathers of the hamlet sleep. — GRAY.

4. I bring fresh showers for the thirsting flowers. — SHELLEY.

5. Strong reasons make strong actions. — SHAKESPEARE.

6. I stood in Venice, on the Bridge of Sighs. — BYRON.

7. I now bade a reluctant farewell to the old hall. — IRVING.

8. A great deal of talent is lost in the world for the want of a little courage. — SIDNEY SMITH.

---

* A briefer method of parsing may be followed as soon as the pupil is familiar with the different steps; thus, *Eyes* is a noun, common, plural, neuter, nominative, and subject of the verb *sparkled*.

EXERCISE II.

1. The eyes of the sleepers waxed deadly and chill. — Byron.

2. Is Saul also among the prophets? — Bible.

3. The doe lifted her head a little with a quick motion, and turned her ear to the south. — C. D. Warner.

4. They had now reached the road which turns off to Sleepy Hollow; but Gunpowder, who seemed possessed with a demon, instead of keeping up it, made an opposite turn, and plunged headlong down hill to the left. — Irving.

5. 'Tis the middle of night by the castle clock,
   And the owls have awakened the crowing cock.
   — Coleridge.

6. A soft answer turneth away wrath. — Bible.

7. Some have even learned to do without happiness, and instead thereof have found blessedness. — Carlyle.

8. The lowing herd winds slowly o'er the lea. — Gray.

9. Reading maketh a full man, conversation a ready man, and writing an exact man. — Bacon.

10. Charity beareth all things, believeth all things, hopeth all things, endureth all things. — Bible.

LESSON XXII.

REVIEW OF NOUNS.

What is a noun? Mention the two leading classes of nouns and state the difference between these classes. What is a collective noun? What is an abstract noun? State three ways in which abstract nouns are formed, and illustrate by examples.

What is meant by inflection? To what do the inflections of nouns relate?

How do most nouns form the plural? Mention other ways in which nouns form their plurals, and illustrate by example.

Give the plural of *watch, piano, potato, donkey, lily, loaf, roof, tooth, ox, sheep.*

Distinguish between the meaning of *brothers* and *brethren; fishes* and *fish; indexes* and *indices; pennies* and *pence.*

State three ways in which compound nouns form the plural, and illustrate by examples.

Give the plural of *larva, alumnus, axis, beau, bandit, seraph.* Why do these nouns not form their plurals in the usual way?

What is gender? How many genders are there, and what does each denote? Mention three ways in which the gender of nouns is distinguished.

Give the feminine nouns corresponding to the nouns *hart, monk, nephew, host, master, governor, executor, hero, man-servant.*

Tell the gender of the nouns *woman, heiress, landlord, doe, waitress, czar, administratrix, guest, friend, witness, cousin, sun, wind, table, house.*

How many cases have nouns? What determines the case of a noun? Which case has a special form? How is the possessive case of nouns formed? How is the possessive formed in compound words and phrases? How may possession be indicated without the possessive form? When is this way preferable?

LESSON XXIII.

PERSONAL PRONOUNS.

Mention the pronouns in the following sentences, and tell which denote the person speaking, which the person spoken to, and which the person or thing spoken of: —

1.   I met a little cottage girl;
    She was eight years old, she said.

2. You will be surprised when you read the report.

3. He requested that we should be present.

4. Buy the truth, and sell it not.

A pronoun that shows by its form whether the person speaking is meant, the person spoken to, or the person or thing spoken of, is called a **personal pronoun**.

A pronoun that denotes the person speaking is said to be in the **first person**; as, *I, we*.

A pronoun that denotes a person spoken to is said to be in the **second person**; as, *thou, ye, you*.

A pronoun that denotes a person or a thing spoken of is said to be in the **third person**; as, *he, she, it, they*.

DECLENSION OF THE PERSONAL PRONOUNS.

FIRST PERSON.

	SINGULAR.		PLURAL.
Nom.	I,	*Nom.*	we,
Poss.	mine, *or* my,	*Poss.*	ours, *or* our,
Obj.	me.	*Obj.*	us.

SECOND PERSON.

	SINGULAR.		PLURAL.
Nom.	thou,	*Nom.*	ye, *or* you,
Poss.	thine, *or* thy,	*Poss.*	yours, *or* your,
Obj.	thee.	*Obj.*	you.

The second person singular is no longer in common use. It is now chiefly used in prayer and in poetry; as, —

1. Withhold not *thou thy* tender mercies from me.

2. I see in *thy* gentle eyes a tear;
    They turn to me in sorrowful thought;
Thou thinkest of friends, the good and dear,
    Who were for a time, and now are not. — BRYANT.

The plural pronoun *you* is used, in ordinary speech, whether one or more than one person is addressed; as, —

1. *You* are merry, my lord. — SHAKESPEARE.

2. *You* are not wood, *you* are not stones, but men. — SHAKESPEARE.

THIRD PERSON.

	SINGULAR.			PLURAL.
	Masc.	*Fem.*	*Neut.*	*Masc., Fem., or Neut.*
Nom.	he,	she,	it,	they,
Poss.	his,	hers, *or* her,	its,	theirs, *or* their,
Obj.	him,	her,	it.	them.

The pronoun of the masculine gender is generally used to refer to a noun which may denote a person of either sex; as, —

Each pupil must provide *his* own material.

The pronoun of the masculine gender is also used in referring to animals or things that are supposed to possess masculine qualities, and the pronoun of the feminine gender is used in referring to animals or things to which feminine qualities are attributed; as,—

1. The *eagle* soars above *his* nest.
2. *Earth*, with *her* thousand voices, praises God. — COLERIDGE.

The pronoun of the neuter gender is often used to refer to animals or to young children, in cases where the sex is not considered; as,—

> The deer raised *its* head.
> The infant knew *its* name.

The possessive forms *my, thy, her, our, your,* and *their* are used with nouns, and the forms *mine, thine, hers, ours, yours,* and *theirs* are used when no noun follows the possessive; as,—

> This is *my* book.
> This book is *mine*.

Mine and *thine* are sometimes used for *my, thy,* before words beginning with a vowel sound; as,—

> Bow down *thine* ear.
> I will lift up *mine* eyes unto the hills.

COMPOUND PERSONAL PRONOUNS.

Tell how the italicized pronouns in the following sentences are formed, and how each is used:—

1. The boy hurt *himself*.
2. We often deceive *ourselves*.
3. I *myself* heard the remark.

The pronouns *my, our, thy, your, him, her, it,* and *them* are used with *self* or *selves* to form **compound personal pronouns.**

These compound pronouns are sometimes used as **reflexives,** that is, as objects denoting the same person or thing as the subject of the verb; as, —

I let *myself* down with a rope.

They are also used to express **emphasis;** as, —

She *herself* read the book.

COMPOUND PERSONAL PRONOUNS.

	Singular.	Plural.
First Person.	myself,	ourselves,
Second Person.	{ thyself, yourself,	yourselves,
Third Person.	{ himself, herself, itself.	themselves.

EXERCISE I.

Tell the person, number, gender, and case of each pronoun in the following exercises: —

1. Something frightened the little animal, and it scampered far away through the woods.

2. I listened with suspended breath, but not a sound came to my ears.

3. Then they praised him, soft and low. — TENNYSON.

4. My son, if sinners entice thee, consent thou not. — BIBLE.

5. He then led me to the highest pinnacle of the rock. — ADDISON.

6. Give every man thine ear, but few thy voice. — SHAKESPEARE.

7. It is excellent discipline for an author to feel that he must say all he has to say in the fewest possible words. — RUSKIN.

8. Boast not thyself of to-morrow;

For thou knowest not what a day may bring forth.

— BIBLE.

LESSON XXIV.

ADJECTIVE PRONOUNS.

Which of the italicized words below are used as adjectives? Which are used as pronouns? —

1. *Many* tickets were sold.
2. *Many* were unable to secure seats.
3. Look at *this* clock.
4. *This* is sold.

Certain words can be used to limit nouns or to stand for nouns. When such words are used with nouns, they are called adjectives; when they stand for nouns they are called **adjective pronouns.** Sometimes there is a difference of form; as, *no* (adj.), *none* (pro.); *other* (adj.), *others* (pro.).

The principal words used as adjective pronouns are *all, another, any, both, each, either, few, many, neither, none, one, other, several, some, this, these, that, those.*

Tell whether the italicized words in the following sentences are adjectives or pronouns, giving reasons in each case:—

1. *Many*, alas! had fallen in battle. — HAWTHORNE.

2. There is a calm for *those* who weep. — J. MONTGOMERY.

3.   *All* are architects of fate,
        Working in *these* walls of time —
   Some with massive deeds and great,
        Some with ornaments of rhyme. — LONGFELLOW.

4. *Any* life that is worth living must be a struggle. — DEAN STANLEY.

5. The man deserving the name is *one* whose thoughts and exertions are for *others* rather than for himself. — SIR WALTER SCOTT.

6. *All* men think *all* men mortal but themselves. — YOUNG.

7. Men at *some* time are masters of their fate. — SHAKESPEARE.

8. *This* was the noblest Roman of them all. — SHAKESPEARE.

9. My worthy friend Sir Roger is *one* of *those* who is not only at peace with himself, but beloved and esteemed by *all* about him. — ADDISON.

10. It is *one* thing to be well informed; it is *another* to be wise. — ROBERTSON.

11. We too seldom think how much we owe to *those* formidable savages. — JOHN FISKE.

12. *Few* shall part where *many* meet. — CAMPBELL.

13.   To know
   That which before us lies in daily life
   Is the prime wisdom. — MILTON.

EXERCISE II.

Construct sentences containing the following words used (1) *as adjectives,* (2) *as adjective pronouns :* —

both,	each,	few,	several,	these,
neither,	none,	many,	that,	other.

LESSON XXV.

RELATIVE PRONOUNS.

Tell how many assertions are made in each of the following sentences, read the principal statement, and state the office of the italicized part : —

1. We found a guide, *who answered our questions.*
2. The wind, *which rose suddenly*, had now ceased.
3. A city *that is set on a hill* cannot be hid.

A part of a sentence that contains a subject and a predicate is called a **clause.**

The clause that expresses the leading or principal thought of a sentence is called an **independent** or **principal clause.**

A clause that depends upon some other part of the sentence for its full meaning is called a **dependent** or **subordinate clause.**

Which words in the dependent clauses above refer to preceding nouns, and how are the dependent clauses joined to the independent clauses?

A word that refers to a preceding noun or pronoun, and connects with it a dependent clause, is called a **relative pronoun.**

The word to which a pronoun refers or relates is called its **antecedent.** The relative pronoun connects the clause of which it is a part to its antecedent.

The relative pronouns are *who, which, that,* and *what.*

Who is applied to persons ; as, —

Hail to the chief *who* in triumph advances. — Scott.

Which is applied to the lower animals and to things without life ; as, —

1. Here is the horse *which* will take us to the end of our journey.

2. Nature has, indeed, given us a soil *which* yields bounteously to the hands of industry. — Webster.

Which was formerly used in speaking of persons; as, —

Our Father *which* art in heaven.

That is applied to persons, to animals, and to things ; as, —

1. Thrice is he armed *that* hath his quarrel just. — Shakespeare.

2. A half-starved dog, *that* looked like Wolf, was skulking about the house. — Irving.

3. A city *that* is set on a hill cannot be hid. — Bible.

What is used without an antecedent expressed. It is equivalent to *that which;* as, —

She remembers *what* [that which] she reads.

As is sometimes used as a relative pronoun. It is then usually preceded by *such;* as, —

Let such *as* [those who] hear take heed.

But is also used as a relative pronoun. It has a negative force ; as, —

> There is no fireside, howsoe'er defended,
> *But* has [*that* has *not*] one vacant chair. — LONGFELLOW.

A relative clause may introduce an additional fact about the antecedent ; as, —

> They had one son, *who had grown up to be the staff and pride of their age.* — IRVING.

Or it may limit or restrict the meaning of the antecedent ; as, —

> The bird *that soars on highest wing*
> Builds on the ground her lowly nest.

That is preferred to *who* in restrictive clauses.
Who is declined as follows : —

SINGULAR OR PLURAL.

Nominative Case.	who,
Possessive Case.	whose,
Objective Case.	whom.

The other relative pronouns are not declined, but *whose* is often used as if it were the possessive form of *which;* as, —

> Bordered with trees *whose* gay leaves fly. — BRYANT.

COMPOUND RELATIVE PRONOUNS.

Pronouns formed by adding *ever* or *soever* to *who, which,* and *what* are called **compound relative pronouns** ; as, *whoever, whosoever; whichever, whichsoever; whatever, whatsoever.*

EXERCISE L

Mention the relative pronouns in the following sentences, name their antecedents, tell what the pronouns connect, and give the case of each : —

1. He that lacks time to mourn lacks time to mend.

2. Where lies the land to which the ship would go?

3. My ramble soon led me to the church, which stood a little distance from the village. — IRVING.

4. What a man has learnt is of importance, but what he is, what he can do, what he will become, are more significant things. — HELPS.

5. He that is slow to anger is better than the mighty. — BIBLE.

6. A land that will not yield satisfactorily without irrigation, and whose best paying produce requires intelligent as well as careful husbandry, will never be an idle land. — WARNER.

7.   All precious things, discovered late,
     To those that seek them issue forth. — TENNYSON.

8.   They are slaves who dare not be
     In the right with two or three. — LOWELL.

9. Here, then, I parted, sorrowfully, from the companion with whom I set out on my journey. — HOLMES.

10. He who has sought renown about the world, and has reaped a full harvest of worldly favor, will find, after all, that there is no love, no admiration, no applause, so sweet to the soul as that which springs up in his native place. — IRVING.

EXERCISE II.

Point out the relative pronouns in the following sentences, name their antecedents, and tell whether the relative clauses introduce additional facts about the antecedents, or limit and restrict their meaning.

1. He that is not with me is against me.

2. The man who provides a home for a poor neighbor is a greater benefactor of the poor than he who lays the foundation of a stately almshouse and never finishes a single apartment. — J. HAMILTON.

3. Those who live without a plan have never any leisure.

4. The Carrier, who had turned his face from the door, signed to him to go if he would. — DICKENS.

5. Carefully then were covered the embers that glowed on the hearth-stone. — LONGFELLOW.

6. Not far from the gateway they came to a bridge, which seemed to be built of iron. — HAWTHORNE

7. The first spring wild-flowers, whose shy faces among the dry leaves and rocks are so welcome, yield no honey. — JOHN BURROUGHS.

8. The tongue is like a race-horse, which runs the faster the less weight it carries. — ADDISON.

9.   We were the first that ever burst
        Into that silent sea. — COLERIDGE.

10.   Bordered with trees whose gay leaves fly
        On every breath that sweeps the sky
        The fresh dark acres furrowed lie,
           And ask the sower's hand. — BRYANT.

A relative pronoun has the same person, number, and gender as its antecedent; as, —

1.
And will your mother pity me,
Who am a maiden most forlorn? — COLERIDGE.

2.
He prayeth best, *who* loveth best
All things, both great and small. — COLERIDGE.

EXERCISE III.

Mention the person, number, gender, and case of each relative pronoun in the following sentences: —

1. Hail to the chief who in triumph advances. — SCOTT.

2. The books which help you most are those which make you think most. — PARKER.

3. They never fail who die in a great cause. — BYRON.

4. The Upper Lake discharges itself into the Lower by a brook which winds through a mile and a half of swamp and woods. — WARNER.

5. I tell you that which you yourselves do know. — SHAKESPEARE.

6. How beautiful upon the mountains are the feet of him that bringeth good tidings! — BIBLE.

7. Where are the flowers, the fair young flowers, that lately sprang and stood
In brighter light, and softer air, a beauteous sisterhood?

8. The charities that soothe and heal and bless,
Lie scattered at the feet of men like flowers.

LESSON XXVI.

INTERROGATIVE PRONOUNS.

How are the italicized words used in the following sentences: —

    1. *Who* comes here?
    2. *Which* reached home first?
    3. *What* is the news?

A pronoun used in asking a question is called an **interrogative pronoun.** The interrogative pronouns are *who, which,* and *what.*

Who refers to persons. It is declined like the relative **who.**

Which refers to persons or to things. It implies selection; as, —

> *Which* of the brothers sings?
> *Which* of the chairs do you prefer?

What refers to things; as, —

> *What* was in the box?

Which and *what* are sometimes used as **interrogative adjectives**; as, —

> Where are they now? *What* lands and skies
> Paint pictures in their friendly eyes?
> *What* hope deludes, *what* promise cheers,
> *What* pleasant voices fill their ears? — LONGFELLOW.

EXERCISE I.

Point out the pronouns in the following sentences, tell the kind of each pronoun, and name its case: —

    1. Who can understand his errors?
    2. The child sat silent beneath a tree, hushed in her

very breath by the stillness of the night, and all its attendant wonders. — DICKENS.

3. Nearly all the most charming of the singing-birds prefer the early morning and the evening twilight for their vocal performances, though some of them sing far into the night. — M. THOMPSON.

4. The stranger at my fireside cannot see
    The forms I see nor hear the sounds I hear;
He but perceives what is; while unto me
    All that has been is visible and clear. — LONGFELLOW.

5. All things that are on earth shall wholly pass away,
Except the love of God, which shall live and last for aye.

6. He is the freeman whom the truth makes free. — COWPER.

7. Ah! what is that sound which now bursts on his ear? — DIMOND.

8. Who, among the whole chattering crowd, can tell me of the forms and the precipices of the chain of tall white mountains that girded the horizon at noon yesterday? Who saw the narrow sunbeam that came out of the south, and smote upon their summits until they melted and mouldered away in a dust of blue rain? Who saw the dance of the dead clouds when the sunlight left them last night, and the west wind blew them before it like withered leaves? — RUSKIN.

EXERCISE II.

Write sentences containing —

1. *Who* used as a relative pronoun in the nominative case; as a relative pronoun in the possessive case; as a rel-

ative pronoun in the objective case; as an interrogative pronoun.

2. *Which* used as an adjective; as a relative pronoun; as an interrogative pronoun.

3. *What* used as an adjective; as a relative pronoun; as an interrogative pronoun.

4. *That* used as an adjective; as an adjective pronoun; as a relative pronoun.

LESSON XXVII.

REVIEW OF PRONOUNS.

EXERCISE L

What is a pronoun? How does a pronoun differ from a noun?

Mention the different classes of pronouns and give examples of each class.

·What is a personal pronoun? How many case forms has the pronoun of the first person? How is each used?

Mention the second person singular, and tell how it is used. Give two uses of the pronoun *you.*

Which person has a distinction of gender? State special uses of the pronouns of the masculine, feminine, and neuter genders. How are the possessive forms of personal pronouns used?

Mention the compound personal pronouns, and tell how they are formed.

Give an example of their use as *reflexives;* for *emphasis.*

How does an adjective pronoun differ from an adjective?

Define a relative pronoun. State the distinctions in the use of *who, which,* and *what.* Give a sentence in which *as* is used as a relative pronoun ; in which *but* is so used.

What is an interrogative pronoun? Name the interrogative pronouns.

EXERCISE II.

Parse the pronouns in the following sentences: —

To parse a pronoun, tell —

1. The **kind** of pronoun.
2. Its **person.**
3. Its **number.**
4. Its **gender.**
5. Its **case.**
6. Its **construction.**

Example.—And then *I* think of *one who* in *her* youthful beauty died.

1. *I* is a personal pronoun, first person, singular number, common gender, nominative case, subject of the verb *think.**

2. *One* is an adjective pronoun, third person, singular number, feminine gender, objective case, object of the preposition *of.*

3. *Who* is a relative pronoun, third person, singular number, feminine gender, agreeing with its antecedent *one,* and nominative case, subject to the verb *died.*

4. *Her* is a personal pronoun, third person, singular number, feminine gender, possessive case, depending upon the noun *beauty.*

1. The moon did not rise till after ten, so I had two hours of intense darkness during which I used my ears instead of my eyes. — M. THOMPSON.

---

* Or follow a briefer form, similar to the one suggested on p. 46.

2. And what is so rare as a day in June? — LOWELL. ·

3. Hang around your walls pictures which shall tell stories of mercy, hope, courage, faith, and charity. — D. G. MITCHELL.

4. A few hoped, and many feared, that some scheme of monarchy would be established. — JOHN FISKE.

5.
    With merry songs we mock the wind
      That in the pine top grieves,
    And slumber long and sweetly
      On beds of oaken leaves. — BRYANT.

6. I witnessed a striking incident in bird life which was very suggestive. — M. THOMPSON.

7. Hast thou a charm to stay the morning star? — COLERIDGE.

8. He laid him down and closed his eyes. — SOUTHEY.

9.
    Triumphant arch, that fill'st the sky
      When storms prepare to part,
    I ask not proud Philosophy
      To teach me what thou art. — CAMPBELL.

10.
    He that only rules by terror
      Doeth grievous wrong. — TENNYSON.

11. We judge ourselves by what we feel capable of doing, while others judge us by what we have already done. — LONG-FELLOW.

12.
    I fear thee, ancient mariner!
    I fear thy skinny hand!
    And thou art long, and lank, and brown,
    As is the ribbed sea-sand. — COLERIDGE.

13. Some are born great, some achieve greatness, and some have greatness thrust upon them. — SHAKESPEARE.

14. He who plants an oak looks forward to future ages, and plants for posterity. — IRVING.

15. Which of us shall be the soonest folded to that dim Unknown?
Which shall leave the other walking in this flinty path alone? — BRYANT.

LESSON XXVIII.

CLASSES OF ADJECTIVES.

Point out the adjectives in the following sentences, and tell what each expresses : —

1. I bring fresh showers for the thirsting flowers.
2. The sun is warm, the sky is clear.
3. A little leaven leaveneth the whole lump.
4. Three years she grew in sun and shower.

An adjective that expresses quality or kind is a **descriptive adjective**; as, a *happy* boy; a *narrow* path; a *wooden* bench.

Descriptive adjectives that are formed from proper nouns are called **proper adjectives**. Tney begin with capital letters; as, *American* forests; the *English* language.

An adjective that points out or denotes number or quantity is a **limiting adjective**; as, *this* week; *two* hours; *much* trouble.

A limiting adjective may be used —

1. Simply to point out; as, *this, that, the, an, yon, yonder*.

2. To express a definite number; as, *one, two, fourteen, fifty.*

3. To express an indefinite number or quantity; as, *any, little, much, many, some.*

4. To show in what order things are arranged; as, *first, second, third.*

The adjectives *the* and *an* or *a* (the shortened form of *an*) are sometimes called **articles**. *The* is called the **definite article.** *An* or *a* is called the **indefinite article.**

The is used to point out some particular person or thing.

An or *a* is used to point out any one person or thing of a class.

An is used before a word beginning with a vowel sound; as, *an* apple; *an* initial; *an* hour (*h* is silent).

A is used before a word beginning with a consonant sound; as, *a* boat; *a* day; many *a* one (*one* begins with the consonant sound of *w*); *a* unit (*unit* begins with the consonant sound of *y*).

An adjective formed from two simple words is called a **compound adjective**; as, —

He turned the *well-worn* leaves.

EXERCISE I.

Point out the adjectives in the following sentences, state the office of each, and tell what kind of adjective it is: —

1. Thirty-two statues of various sizes were found in this field.

2. Its chief attractions were a never-failing breeze at night, good water, and a large garden in the centre of a cleared space.

3. Hark! 'tis the twanging horn o'er yonder bridge. — COWPER.

4. We met several men riding at a rapid pace.

5.   Across its antique portico
       Tall poplar trees their shadows throw. — LONGFELLOW.

6. This long march through the primeval forest and over rugged and trackless mountains was one of the most remarkable exploits of the war. — JOHN FISKE.

7. O blessings on his kindly voice and on his silver hair! — TENNYSON.

8. Suddenly there was a gentle little tap on the inside of the lid. — HAWTHORNE

9. The thirteen colonies were now free and independent States. — HAWTHORNE.

10. A certain man fell among thieves. — BIBLE.

11. Small service is true service while it lasts. — WORDSWORTH.

12. All the air a solemn stillness holds. — GRAY.

13.   With a slow and noiseless footstep
        Comes that messenger divine. — LONGFELLOW.

14.   With fingers weary and worn,
            With eyelids heavy and red,
        A woman sat, in unwomanly rags,
            Plying her needle and thread. — HOOD.

15.   All the little boys and girls,
        With rosy cheeks and flaxen curls,
        And sparkling eyes and teeth like pearls,
        Tripping and skipping, ran merrily after
        The wonderful music with shouting and laughter.
                                        — BROWNING.

EXERCISE II.

Tell whether an or a should be used before each of the following words: —

hammock,	image,	hour,	youth,
poem,	bird,	mountain,	honor,
author,	instant,	eagle,	useful,
errand,	union,	orange,	one.

EXERCISE III.

Write sentences containing the following words used as adjectives: —

strong,	any,	many,	brittle,	prompt,
fair,	all,	curved,	every,	distant,
both,	dutiful,	little,	modern,	neither,
some,	few,	much,	each,	another,
clear,	brief,	certain,	other,	several.

LESSON XXIX.

COMPARISON OF ADJECTIVES.

Tell how many forms the adjective *long* has in the following sentences, and what each form expresses : —

1. This work requires a long pencil.
2. Your pencil is longer than mine.
3. Here is the longest pencil in the box.

Adjectives have different forms to express different **degrees of quality**. This change of form is called **comparison**.

The form of an adjective that simply expresses the quality is called the **positive degree**; as, *long, short*.

The form of an adjective that expresses a higher or a lower degree of the quality is called the **comparative degree**; as, *longer, shorter*.

The comparative degree is used in comparing two things or classes of things; as, Charles is *older* than Ralph; Pears are *dearer* than apples.

The form of an adjective that expresses the highest or the lowest degree of the quality is called the **superlative degree**; as, *longest, shortest*.

The superlative degree is used in comparing one thing with all others of the same kind; as, Charles is the *oldest* boy in his class.

Most adjectives of one syllable add *er* to the simple form of the adjective, to form the comparative, and *est*, to form the superlative. If the adjective ends in *e*, one *e* is omitted; as, —

POSITIVE.	COMPARATIVE.	SUPERLATIVE.
long,	*longer,*	*longest.*
wise,	*wiser,*	*wisest.*

Most adjectives of more than one syllable prefix *more* or *less* to the simple form of the adjective, to form the comparative, and *most* or *least*, to form the superlative; as, —

POSITIVE.	COMPARATIVE.	SUPERLATIVE.
careful,	*more careful,*	*most careful.*
fortunate,	*less fortunate,*	*least fortunate.*

A few adjectives of two syllables, ending in sounds that unite easily with the sound of *er* or *est*, may be compared by adding *er* or *est;* as, *noble, happy, narrow, tender, pleasant.*

The following adjectives are compared irregularly :—

POSITIVE.	COMPARATIVE.	SUPERLATIVE.
bad, ill,	worse,	worst.
far,	farther,	farthest.
[forth,]	further,	furthest. furthermost.
fore,	former,	foremost. first.
good,	better,	best.
late,	later, latter,	latest. last.
little,	less,	least.
many, much,	more,	most.
old,	elder, older,	eldest. oldest.

The two adjectives *this* and *that* are inflected for number; thus,—

SINGULAR.	PLURAL.
this,	these.
that,	those.

EXERCISE I.

Mention each adjective in the following sentences, name its degree, and tell what it modifies: —

1. Choose the timbers with greatest care. — LONGFELLOW.

2. Of all the old festivals, however, that of Christmas awakens the strongest and most heartfelt associations. — IRVING.

3. He who ascends to mountain tops shall find
The loftiest peaks most wrapt in clouds and snow.
— BRYANT.

4. The edges and corners of the box were carved with most wonderful skill. — HAWTHORNE.

5. She is more precious than rubies. — BIBLE.

6. We started immediately after an early luncheon, followed an excellent road all the way, and were back in time for dinner at half-past six.

7. The day was cloudy, and the sea very rough.

8.   Alas! when evil men are strong,
No life is good, no pleasure long. — WORDSWORTH.

9. He that is slow to anger is better than the mighty. — BIBLE.

10. The noblest mind the best contentment has. — SPENSER.

11. This was the noblest Roman of them all. — SHAKESPEARE.

12. The greatest man is he who chooses the right with invincible resolution; who resists the sorest temptations from within and from without; who bears the heaviest burdens cheerfully; who is calmest and most fearless under menaces and frowns; whose reliance on truth, on virtue, on God, is most unfaltering. — CHANNING.

EXERCISE II.

Write the comparison of the following adjectives: —

narrow,	noble,	deep,	famous,	ancient,
beautiful,	clear,	swift,	good,	expensive,
generous,	distant,	formal,	cheerful,	earnest,
lofty,	merry,	heavy,	near,	attractive,
lovely,	brief,	many,	bad,	little.

Examples.—POSITIVE.	COMPARATIVE.	SUPERLATIVE.
noble,	nobler,	noblest.
generous,	more generous,	most generous.

———

LESSON XXX.

REVIEW OF ADJECTIVES.

EXERCISE I.

What is an adjective? Into what two classes may adjectives be divided?

Name three adjectives that are used to point out things; two adjectives that express a definite number; two that express an indefinite number; two that express an indefinite quantity; two that indicate order of arrangement.

State the difference in meaning between *the* and *an* or *a*. Distinguish between the use of *an* and *a*, and illustrate by examples.

Name two adjectives that change their form to denote the plural number. Give their plural forms.

What is meant by the comparison of adjectives? What are the

three degrees of comparison called? Define each, and give an example.

How is the comparative formed? Give examples. How is the superlative formed? Give examples.

What is meant by irregular comparison? Illustrate.

Mention two adjectives that are compared by means of suffixes; two by means of adverbs; two that are compared irregularly; and two that are not usually compared.

Give the comparative and superlative forms of *few; heavy; amiable; swift; useful; fierce; mighty; witty; gentle; good; bad; late; little; ill; much; many.*

EXERCISE II.

Parse the adjectives in the following sentences: —

To parse an adjective, tell —

1. The **kind** of adjective.
2. Its **degree**, if the adjective can be compared.
3. Its **construction**.

Example. — *The* wind was *cold.*

1. *The* is a specifying adjective, modifying the noun *wind.*
2. *Cold* is a descriptive adjective of the positive degree. It completes the meaning of the verb *was*, and modifies the noun *wind.*

1. It is the most beautiful shrub that ever sprang out of the earth.

2. Every good tree bringeth forth good fruit, but a corrupt tree bringeth forth evil fruit.

3.　　Such pleasures nerve the arm for strife,
　　　Bring joyous thoughts and golden dreams.

4. This door led into a passage out of which opened four sleeping-rooms.

5. Wide is the gate, and broad is the way.

6. In the middle of the eighteenth century there were four New England colonies. — Fiske.

7. Birds of the polar areas of snow and ice are white, those of the tropics are vari-colored and brilliant-hued. — M. Thompson.

8. Straight and strong and magnificently plumed, the palms rose to an average height of seventy or eighty feet. — A. B. Edwards.

9. Spring is the season when the volume of bird-song poured round the world is incomparably stronger, fuller, and sweeter than at any other. — M. Thompson.

10.　　Lo! while we are gazing, in swifter haste
　　　Stream down the snows, till the air is white.
　　　　　　　　　　　　　　　　　　— Bryant.

11. The habit of observation is the habit of clear and decisive gazing. Not by a first casual glance, but by a steady deliberate aim of the eye are the rare and characteristic things discovered. — John Burroughs.

12.　　A form more fair, a face more sweet,
　　　Ne'er hath it been my lot to meet. — Whittier

13. A beautiful form is better than a beautiful face; a beautiful behavior is better than a beautiful form: it gives a higher pleasure than statues or pictures; it is the finest of the fine arts. — Emerson.

LESSON XXXI.

TRANSITIVE AND INTRANSITIVE VERBS.

Point out the verb in each of the following sentences, name its subject,* and tell which word limits the action expressed by the verb : —

1. The sexton rang the bell.
2. A boy delivered the message.
3. The frost killed the plant.

The noun or pronoun that limits the action expressed by a verb is the **object*** of the verb; as, We crossed the *bridge*.

Tell which verbs in the following sentences take objects to complete their meaning, and which do not take objects : —

1. The traveller sold his horse.
2. Bees gather honey.
3. The sun shines.
4. The ship sailed.

A verb that takes an object is called a **transitive verb**; as, Henry *threw* the ball.

A verb that does not take an object is called an **intransitive verb**; as, Birds *fly*.

The same word may be used as a transitive verb in one sentence, and as an intransitive verb in another; as, —

The wind blows the dust. (Transitive.)
The wind blows. (Intransitive.)

---

* These terms as applied to nouns refer to what is called the *grammatical* or *bare* subject, and object, and not to the *logical* or *complete* subject, and object.

Some intransitive verbs have a complete meaning in themselves; as, —

The rain falls.

Other intransitive verbs must be followed by a noun or an adjective to complete their meaning; as, —

1. He *was* a statesman.
2. The day *is* cloudy.

EXERCISE I.

Select the transitive verbs, and name the subject and the object of each: —

1. He shrugged his shoulders, shook his head, cast up his eyes, but said nothing. — IRVING.
2. Each takes his seat, and each receives his share.
3. We scatter seeds with careless hand.
4. Can the blind lead the blind? — BIBLE.
5. Do many good works, and speak few vanities. — CHAUCER.

6. We carved not a line, and we raised not a stone,
    But we left him alone in his glory. — WOLFE.

7. The heavens declare the glory of God, and the firmament showeth his handiwork. — BIBLE.
8. The warrior bowed his crested head. — HEMANS.
9. The doe lifted her head a little with a quick motion, and turned her ear to the south. Had she heard something? — C. D. WARNER.

10. In the cold moist earth we laid her, when the forests
     cast the leaf,
     And we wept that one so lovely should have a life
     so brief. — BRYANT.

EXERCISE II.

Tell whether the verbs in the following sentences are transitive or intransitive, mention the objects of the transitive verbs, and tell what complete the meanings of the incomplete intransitive verbs : —

1. A tear stood in his bright blue eye. — LONGFELLOW.
2. A rill of water trickles down the cliff. — HAWTHORNE.
3. The Piper advanced, and the children followed. — BROWNING.
4. My heart leaps up when I behold a rainbow in the sky. — WORDSWORTH.
5. The daffodil is our doorside queen. — BRYANT.
6. The next day Congress took the formal vote upon the resolution. — FISKE.
7. Behold the fowls of the air. — BIBLE.

8. The fish swam by the castle wall,
     And they seemed joyous, each and all. — BYRON.

9. Open then I flung the shutter, when, with many a
     flirt and flutter,
     In there stepped a stately raven of the saintly days
     of yore. — POE.

10. The fair breeze blew, the white foam flew. — COLERIDGE.

EXERCISE III.

Write sentences containing the following words used as transitive verbs : —

learn,	drink,	write,	watch,	set,
speaks,	saw,	flew,	raise,	lay.

EXERCISE IV.

Write sentences containing the following words used as intransitive verbs : —

roar,	grow,	fall,	write,	watch,
speaks,	lie,	sit,	rise,	flew.

LESSON XXXII.

ACTIVE AND PASSIVE VOICE.

Tell in how many ways each thought is expressed in the following sentences : —

1. The governor signed the bill.
2. The bill was signed by the governor.
3. A hound chased the deer.
4. The deer was chased by a hound.

A transitive verb may represent its subject as acting or as being acted upon.

A transitive verb that represents its subject as acting is said to be in the **active voice**; as, Columbus *discovered* America.

A transitive verb that represents its subject as being acted upon is said to be in the **passive voice**; as, America *was discovered* by Columbus.

The object of the verb in the active form becomes the subject of the verb in the passive form. The active voice makes the agent prominent, while the passive voice makes the object of the action prominent.

Some verbs usually intransitive become transitive by means of a preposition, and take the passive voice; as, —

He *disposed of* the goods.
The goods *were disposed of* by him.

EXERCISE L.

Tell the voice of each transitive verb in the following sentences, giving in each case a reason for your statement: —

1. The frightened animal sought the open country.
2. Our guide had never visited the cave.
3. The building was destroyed by fire, but some of the furniture was saved.
4. The guest was admitted into the parlor.
5. The portrait attracted his notice at once.
6. The petition was signed by a number of prominent citizens.
7. He holds him with his glittering eye. — COLERIDGE.
8. Many interesting discoveries were made among these broken cliffs. — HAWTHORNE.
9. He shrugged his shoulders, shook his head, cast up his eyes, but said nothing. — IRVING.

10. The farmer swung the scythe or turned the hay,
And 'twixt the heavy swaths his children were at play.
— BRYANT.

11. On Christmas eve the bells were rung. — SCOTT.

12. The schoolmaster swept and smoothed the ground before the door, trimmed the long grass, trained the ivy and creeping plants which hung their drooping heads in melancholy neglect; and gave to the outer walls a cheery air of home. — DICKENS.

EXERCISE II.

Rewrite the sentences in the preceding exercise, changing the voice of each transitive verb.

— ∘ —

LESSON XXXIII.

MODE.

Find in the following sentences a verb that asserts something as a fact, one that asserts something as doubtful, and one that expresses a command : —

1. He speaks distinctly.
2. If he be at home, we shall see him.
3. Speak the truth.

The manner of asserting is called the **mode** of the verb.

A verb that asserts a thing as a fact or asks a direct question is in the **indicative mode**; as, —

The river *is* deep.
Is the river deep?

A verb that expresses something as conditional or doubtful is in the **subjunctive mode**; as, —

> If he *were* ill, he would inform us.
> Take heed, lest thou *fall*.

A verb in the subjunctive mode is generally preceded by *if, though, lest, unless, except,* or some similar word.

The verb in a conditional clause is not always in the subjunctive mode. When the verb expresses doubt or denial it is in the subjunctive mode, but when it expresses certainty it is in the indicative mode; as, —

If the law *be* [Subjunctive] unjust, it should be repealed.
If the law *is* [Indicative] unjust, it must be enforced.

A verb that expresses a command or an entreaty is in the **imperative mode**; as, —

> *Close* the gate.
> *Forgive* us our debts.

EXERCISE I.

Tell what each verb expresses in the following sentences, and name its mode : —

1. Consider the lilies of the field. — BIBLE.
2. The blue smoke widened slowly upward through the quiet August atmosphere. — LOWELL.
3. I stand upon my native hills again.
4. Thine own friend and thy father's friend, forsake not.
5. If you were in my place you would think differently.
6. Though this be madness, yet there is method in't.
7. Turn away thine eyes, lest they behold vanity.
8. Though he slay me, yet will I trust him.

9.   Last night, the moon had a golden ring,
         And to-night no moon we see. — LONGFELLOW.

10. If fortune serve me, I'll requite this kindness. — SHAKESPEARE.

EXERCISE II.

1. *Write three sentences containing verbs in the indicative mode.*

2. *Write three sentences containing verbs in the subjunctive mode.*

3. *Write three sentences containing verbs in the imperative mode.*

LESSON XXXIV.

THE INFINITIVE.

Select from the following sentences forms of verbs that do not assert, but that name actions, like nouns, and tell how they are used : —

1. To err is human.
2. They intend to return soon.
3. Doing nothing is tiresome.

The form of the verb that does not assert but that merely names action or being, like a noun, is called the **infinitive**.

There are two infinitives, the **simple infinitive**, and the **infinitive in ing**.

The simple infinitive is the simple form of the verb alone, or preceded by **to**; as, —

      Let him *go*, I expect *to go*.

The simple form, without to, is used alone, or after a few of the most common verbs, such as *may, can, must, shall, will, bid, dare, do, let, make, need, hear,* and *see;* as, Why flee? Do not flee.

The form with **to** is employed in most of the uses of the simple infinitive.*

The infinitive in **ing**, also called the **participial infinitive** or **gerund**, is formed by adding *ing* to the simple form of the verb; as, —

Learn the luxury of *doing* good.

The infinitive, like a noun, may be used as subject or object; and, like a verb, it may take an object, if transitive, or may have modifiers; as, —

1. *To retreat* is impossible.
2. I decided *to remain* at home.
3. There is no prospect of *finding* the treasure.

EXERCISE I.

Classify the infinitives in the following sentences, giving reasons for your statements: —

1. I like to look on a scene like this.
2. Let music swell the breeze.
3. The rain had ceased to patter, and now began to fall with a steady determination.
4. There was no difficulty in finding the river.
5. But where to find that happiest spot below,
   Who can direct, when all pretend to know? — GOLDSMITH.

---

* *To* was originally a preposition, used with the infinitive only in certain relations. It is now a mere prefix, or sign of the infinitive in most of its uses. As this is the only one of the infinitive forms that is distinctive, it is commonly named as *the infinitive.* The other forms are, however, equally true infinitives in origin and in use

6. A man has no more right to say an uncivil thing than to act one. — DR. JOHNSON.

7. He hears the parson pray and preach. — LONGFELLOW.

8. As he approached the stream, his heart began to thump. — IRVING.

9. But it must be understood that we did not go to see the Pyramids. We went only to look at them. — A. B. EDWARDS.

10. There are two opposite ways by which some men make a figure in the world; one by talking faster than they think, and the other by holding their tongues and not thinking at all. — IRVING.

EXERCISE II.

Write sentences containing (1) *simple infinitives,* (2) *participial infinitives formed from the following verbs:* —

find,	break,	choose,	lose,	sell,
build,	hear,	spend,	meet,	have.

LESSON XXXV.

THE PARTICIPLE.

Tell of what verbs the italicized words are forms, and which parts of speech they most resemble : —

1. Out came the children *running*.

2. We beheld a horseman *approaching* leisurely.

3. The company, *seated* round the fire, welcomed the stranger.

4. We sailed by an island *covered* with large trees.

The form of the verb that is part adjective and part verb is called a **participle.** The participle does not assert, but assumes or implies action or being. It qualifies a noun or pronoun, like an adjective, and takes modifiers like a verb. A participle from a transitive verb takes an object.

A participle that denotes unfinished action is called a **present or imperfect participle**; as, *hearing, writing*.

A participle that denotes finished action is called a **past or perfect participle**; as, *heard, written*.

The present participle and the participial infinitive have the same form, but the participle is part verb and part adjective, while the infinitive is part verb and part noun. The verbal noun derived from the verb and the participial adjective also end in ing; as, —

1. He hears his daughter's voice, *singing* [Participle] in the village choir. — LONGFELLOW.

2. They spent the evening in *singing* [Infinitive] carols.

3. The time of the *singing* [Noun] of birds has come. — BIBLE.

4. A *singing* [Adjective] bird on every bough. — HOWITT.

The verbal noun may be distinguished from the participial infinitive by taking an article before it, and by not being followed by an object. The participial adjective may be distinguished from the participle, by expressing not action but quality, and by not taking an object.

EXERCISE I.

Select the participles in the following sentences, mention the kind, and tell what each modifies : —

1. I heard my own mountain goats bleating aloft. — CAMPBELL.

2.   Toiling, — rejoicing, — sorrowing,
      Onward through life he goes. — LONGFELLOW.

3. The passengers, warned by the helmsman, retreated into the cabin. — LOSSING.

4. While I lay musing on my pillow, I heard the sound of little feet pattering outside of the door. — IRVING.

5.   All precious things, discovered late,
      To those that seek them issue forth. — TENNYSON.

6. Heaped in the hollows of the grove, the withered leaves lie dead. — BRYANT.

7. Looking out of the window, I saw a crow perched upon the edge of the nest. — BURROUGHS.

8. Yonder sat a tailor cross-legged, making a waistcoat; near him, stretched on his face at full length, sprawled a basket-maker with his half-woven basket and bundles of rushes beside him; and here, close against the main entrance, lay a blind man and his dog; the master asleep, the dog keeping watch. — AMELIA B. EDWARDS.

9.   Watching their leader's beck and will,
      All silent there they stood, and still. — SCOTT.

10. Truth, crushed to earth, shall rise again. — BRYANT.

EXERCISE II.

1. *Copy from any standard writer ten sentences containing present participles. Underline the participles.*

2. *Copy from any standard writer ten sentences containing past participles.*

EXERCISE III.

Distinguish between the different forms of the verb in ing in the following sentences, and tell how each is used: —

1. The darting swallows soar and sing.

2. After standing a long time at the end of the wharf, gazing seaward, the strangers began to stray into the town.

3. Coming back we met two or three more regiments.

4. I had now given up all expectation of finding the road.

5. One could wander for miles through this forest without meeting a person, or hearing a sound, other than the occasional chatter of a squirrel, the song of a bird, or the sighing of the wind through the branches overhead.

6.   Hark! from the murmuring clods I hear
        Glad voices of the coming year. — BRYANT.

7. There's a merry brown thrush sitting up in a tree. — LUCY LARCOM.

8. But sorrow returned with the dawning of morn,
   And the voice in my dreaming ear melted away.
                                        — CAMPBELL.

EXERCISE IV.

Write sentences containing a form of the verb in ing used —

1. As an infinitive.
2. As a participle.
3. As a noun.
4. As an adjective.

LESSON XXXVI.

TENSE.

Tell what time each verb expresses in the following sentences, and mention the different forms of the verb: —

1. I see the light.
2. I saw the light.
3. I shall see the light.

The form of the verb that expresses the time of the action is called **tense**.

Since there are three divisions of time — present, past, and future, there are three leading tenses — **present, past, and future.**

A verb that denotes present time is in the **present tense**; as, I *hear.*

A verb that denotes past time is in the **past tense**; as, I *heard.*

A verb that denotes future time is in the **future tense**; as, I *shall hear.*

Besides these three leading tenses, there are three **perfect tenses**, which denote action as finished or completed.

A verb that denotes an action as completed at the *present* time is in the **present perfect tense**; as, —

I *have heard* the speaker.
He *has finished* the work.

A verb that denotes an action as having been completed before some *past* time is in the **past perfect tense**; as, —

He *had heard* the report.

A verb that denotes an action to be completed before some future time is in the **future perfect tense**; as, —

I *shall have heard* the lecture.
He *will have heard* the lecture.

FORMATION OF TENSES.

Tell which tenses are indicated by the form of the verb itself, and which are made by the aid of other verbs: —

TENSES OF THE INDICATIVE MODE.

PRESENT.	I *write.*	PRESENT PERFECT.	I *have written.*
PAST.	I *wrote.*	PAST PERFECT.	I *had written.*
FUTURE.	I *shall write.*	FUTURE PERFECT.	I *shall have written.*

Only two tenses, the present and the past, are indicated by the form of the verb itself. The other tenses are expressed by the aid of other verbs, called **auxiliary** verbs.

The future tense is made up of the verb *shall* or *will* and the simple infinitive of the verb expressing the action.

Shall is used in the first person, and *will* in the second and third persons, to announce future action. (See Lesson XL.)

The present-perfect tense is made up of the auxiliary verb *have* and the perfect participle of the principal verb.

The past-perfect tense is made up of the auxiliary verb *had* and the perfect participle of the principal verb.

The future-perfect tense is made up of the auxiliary *shall* or *will* and the perfect infinitive of the verb expressing the action.

EXERCISE I.

Mention the verbs in the following sentences, and name the tense of each: —

1. We started late in the afternoon of the first day.
2. There is a land of pure delight.
3. I had now come in sight of the house.
4. A ship-of-war arrived unexpectedly in the bay.
5. The walls of this most curious and interesting fortress have probably lost much of their original height.
6. Over the sea our galleys went.
7. The moon had risen, but the breeze had dropped.
8. A cuckoo's nest is a very simple affair, but it will bear close study. — M. THOMPSON.
9. Short space he stood, — then waved his hand:
   Down sunk the disappearing band. — SCOTT.
10. It is a strange thing how little in general people know about the sky. — RUSKIN.
11. Other soldiers heard the noise, and ran hastily from the barracks to assist their comrades. — HAWTHORNE.
12.   My heart leaps up when I behold
         A rainbow in the sky:
       So was it when my life began;
       So is it now I am a man. — WORDSWORTH.

EXERCISE II.

Write six tense forms for each of the following verbs, to be used with the subject I: —

find,   break,   come,   drive,   forget,
give,   know,   see,   draw,   sell.

LESSON XXXVII.

PERSON AND NUMBER.

Tell how many forms of the verb *hear* are used with the different subjects in the following, and give the endings of the special forms : —

	SINGULAR.	PLURAL.
First Person.	I hear.	We hear.
Second Person.	Thou hearest.	You hear.
Third Person.	He hears.	They hear.

The different forms that a verb takes to correspond to the person and the number of its subject are called **person** and **number** forms.

The second person singular has the ending *est* or *st* in both the present and past tenses of the indicative mode; as, —

> *Present.* Thou plant*est;* thou see*st.*
> *Past.*   Thou planted*st;* thou saw*st.*

The third person singular has, in the present indicative, the ending *s* or *es* and the old forms *eth* or *th;* as, —

> She sleep*s* or she sleep*eth.*
> He doe*s* or he do*th* or he do*eth.*

The forms with *thou* and the forms in *th* or *eth* are now seldom used, except in prayer and in poetry.

With the exception of the verb *be,* the first person singular and the plural forms for all the persons have no endings to mark person or number.

The verb *be* has different forms for the singular and the plural in the present and past tenses of the indicative mode; as, —

SINGULAR.	PLURAL.
I *am*.	We, you, or they *are*.
I *was*.	We, you, or they *were*.

EXERCISE.

Write the forms of the following verbs required for the subjects **I, thou, he,** *and* **we,** *in the indicative present:* —

draw,	hear,	move,	speak,	sing,
see,	stand,	choose,	lift,	come,
find,	forget,	know,	take,	stand.

LESSON XXXVIII.

FORMS OF VERBS.

Tell how the past tenses of the following verbs are formed : —

PRESENT.	PAST.	PERF. PART.	PRESENT.	PAST.	PERF. PART.
plant,	planted,	planted.	fall,	fell,	fallen.
look,	looked,	looked.	throw,	threw,	thrown.
live,	lived,	lived.	give,	gave,	given.

A verb that forms its past tense by adding *ed* or *d* to the present is a **regular verb**; as, *walk, walked; move, moved.*

A verb that does not form its past tense by adding *ed* or *d* to the present is an **irregular verb**; as, *drive, drove; give, gave.*

Verbs are divided into the **strong** and the **weak conjugations.**

A verb that forms its past tense by changing the vowel of the present, without adding anything to the present, is a **strong verb**; as, *fall, fell; throw, threw.*

The perfect participle of all strong verbs once ended in *en* or *n*, but this suffix has now disappeared from many verbs. As the strong verbs are the oldest verbs in the language, they are said to belong to the **old conjugation.**

A verb that forms its past tense by adding *ed, d,* or *t* to the present is a **weak verb**; as, *walk, walked; move, moved; deal, dealt.*

As the weak verbs include all new verbs and all new forms of old verbs, they are said to belong to the **new conjugation.**

Most weak verbs are regular, but some are irregular; as, —

	PRESENT.	PAST.
REGULAR.	{ *plant,* { *move,*	*planted.* *moved.*
IRREGULAR.	*keep,*	*kept.*

A few weak verbs have both regular and irregular forms; as, *build, builded* or *built; kneel, kneeled* or *knelt.*

Some verbs have both strong and weak forms, or mixed forms; as, —

PRESENT.	PAST.	PERF. PART.
thrive,	{ *throve* [strong], { *thrived* [weak],	*thriven* [strong]. *thrived* [weak].
heave,	{ *hove* [strong], { *heaved* [weak],	*heaved* [weak].
sow,	*sowed* [weak],	{ *sown* [strong]. { *sowed* [weak].

The present tense, the past tense, and the perfect participle are called the **principal parts** of a verb, since all the other parts can be given when these three parts are known.

A verb that lacks any of the principal parts is called **defective**; as, *may, shall.*

LIST OF IRREGULAR VERBS.

I.—IRREGULAR VERBS OF THE OLD CONJUGATION.

PRESENT.	PAST.	PERF. PART.	PRESENT.	PAST.	PERF. PART.
abide,	abode,	abode.	chide,	chid,	{ chidden. / chid.
arise,	arose,	arisen.	choose,	chose,	chosen.
awake,	{ awoke, / *awaked,*	awoke. / *awaked.**	cleave [to split],	{ clove, / *cleft,*	cloven. / *cleft.*
bear [to bring forth],	{ bore,	born.	cling,	clung,	clung.
bear [to carry],	{ bore,	borne.	come,	came,	come.
beat,	beat,	beaten.	dig,	{ dug, / *digged,*	dug. / *digged.*
begin,	began,	begun.	do,	did,	done.
behold,	beheld,	{ beholden. / beheld.	draw,	drew,	drawn.
bid,	{ bade, / bid,	bidden. / bid.	drink,	drank,	{ drunken. / drunk.
bind,	bound,	bound.	drive,	drove,	driven.
bite,	bit,	{ bitten. / bit.	eat,	ate,	eaten.
blow,	blew,	blown.	fall,	fell,	fallen.
break,	broke,	broken.	fight,	fought,	fought.
burst,	burst,	burst.	find,	found,	found.
			fling,	flung,	flung.
			fly,	flew,	flown.

* Forms in Italics are **weak.**

PRESENT.	PAST.	PERF. PART.	PRESENT.	PAST.	PERF. PART.
forbear,	forbore,	forborne.	shrink,	shrank, / shrunk,	shrunken. / shrunk.
forget,	forgot,	forgotten.			
forsake,	forsook,	forsaken.	sing,	sang,	sung.
freeze,	froze,	frozen.	sink,	sank,	sunken. / sunk.
get,	got,	gotten. / got.			
			sit,	sat,	sat.
give,	gave,	given.	slay,	slew,	slain.
go,	*went*,	gone.	slide,	slid,	slidden. / slid.
grind,	ground,	ground.			
grow,	grew,	grown.	sling,	slung,	slung.
hang,	hung, / *hanged*,	hung. / *hanged*.	slink,	slunk,	slunk.
			smite,	smote,	smitten.
heave,	hove, / *heaved*,	*heaved*.	speak,	spoke,	spoken.
			spin,	spun,	spun.
hide,	hid,	hidden. / hid.	spring,	sprang,	sprung.
			stand,	stood,	stood.
hold,	held,	held.	steal,	stole,	stolen.
know,	knew,	known.	sting,	stung,	stung.
lie,	lay,	lain.	stride,	strode,	stridden.
ride,	rode,	ridden.	strike,	struck,	stricken. / struck.
ring,	rang,	rung.			
rise,	rose,	risen.	string,	strung,	strung.
run,	ran,	run.	strive,	strove,	striven.
see,	saw,	seen.	swear,	swore,	sworn.
seethe,	sod, / *seethed*,	sodden. / *seethed*.	swim,	swam,	swum.
			swing,	swung,	swung.
shake,	shook,	shaken.	take,	took,	taken.
shine,	shone,	shone.	tear,	tore,	torn.
shoot,	shot,	shot.			

PRESENT.	PAST.	PERF. PART.	PRESENT.	PAST.	PERF. PART.
thrive,	throve, *thrived*,	thriven. *thrived.*	wear,	wore,	worn.
throw,	threw,	thrown.	weave,	wove,	woven.
tread,	trod,	{ trodden. { trod.	win,	won,	won.
			wind,	wound,	wound.
wake,	{ woke, { *waked*,	} *waked.*	wring,	wrung,	wrung.
			write,	wrote,	written.

EXERCISE I.

Make a list of strong verbs which have different forms for the present tense, the past tense, and the perfect participle.

EXERCISE II.

Make a list of strong verbs which have the same form for the past tense and the perfect participle.

EXERCISE III.

Make a list of verbs which have two different forms for either the past tense or the past participle, or for both.

EXERCISE IV.

Write the principal parts of the following verbs: —

beat,	blow,	choose,	do,	fly,
forget,	freeze,	give,	hold,	know,
lie,	ride,	ring,	see,	sit,
speak,	steal,	swim,	wear,	write,
cleave,	come,	run,	hang,	smite.

II.—IRREGULAR VERBS OF THE NEW CONJUGATION.

PRESENT.	PAST.	PERF. PART.	PRESENT.	PAST.	PERF. PART.
bend,	bent,	bended. bent.	gild,	gilded, gilt,	gilded. gilt.
bereave,	bereaved, bereft.	bereaved. bereft.	gird,	girt,	girt.
			have,	had,	had.
beseech,	besought,	besought.	hear,	heard,	heard.
breed,	bred,	bred.	hide,	hid,	hidden. hid.
bring,	brought,	brought.			
build,	builded, built,	builded. built.	hit,	hit,	hit.
			hurt,	hurt,	hurt.
burn,	burned, burnt.	burned. burnt.	keep,	kept,	kept.
			kneel,	kneeled, knelt,	kneeled. knelt.
buy,	bought,	bought.	knit,	knit,	knit.
cast,	cast,	cast.	lay,	laid,	laid.
catch,	caught,	caught.	lead,	led,	led.
clothe,	clothed, clad,	clothed. clad.	lean,	leaned, leant,	leaned. leant.
cost,	cost,	cost.	leap,	leaped, leapt,	leaped. leapt.
creep,	crept,	crept.			
cut,	cut,	cut.	learn,	learned, learnt,	learned. learnt.
deal,	dealt,	dealt.	leave,	left,	left.
dream,	dreamed, dreamt,	dreamed. dreamt.	lend,	lent,	lent.
			let,	let,	let.
dwell,	dwelled, dwelt,	dwelled. dwelt.	light,	lighted, lit,	lighted. lit.
feed,	fed,	fed.			
feel,	felt,	felt.			
flee,	fled,	fled.	lose,	lost,	lost.

PRESENT.	PAST.	PERF. PART.	PRESENT.	PAST.	PERF. PART.
make,	made,	made.	sleep,	slept,	slept.
mean,	meant,	meant.	slit,	slit,	slit.
meet,	met,	met.	smell,	smelled,	smelled.
pass,	passed,	passed. *past.*		smelt,	smelt.
pay,	paid,	paid.	sow,	sowed,	*sown.* sowed.
pen,	penned, pent,	penned. pent.	speed,	sped,	sped.
put,	put,	put.	spell,	spelled, spelt,	spelled. spelt.
quit,	quitted, quit,	quitted. quit.	spend,	spent,	spent.
read,	read,	read.	spill,	spilt,	spilt.
rend,	rent,	rent.	spread,	spread,	spread.
say,	said,	said.	strew,	strewed,	*strewn.* strewed.
seek,	sought,	sought.	sweat,	sweat,	sweat.
sell,	sold,	sold.	sweep,	swept,	swept.
send,	sent,	sent.	teach,	taught,	taught.
set,	set,	set.	tell,	told,	told.
shed,	shed,	shed.	think,	thought,	thought.
shoe,	shod,	shod.	thrust,	thrust,	thrust.
show,	showed,	*shown.** showed.	weep,	wept,	wept.
shred,	shred,	shred.	wet,	wet,	wet.
shut,	shut,	shut.	work,	wrought, worked,	wrought. worked.

EXERCISE L.

Make a list of irregular weak verbs which change their form for the past tense and the perfect participle.

---

* Forms in Italics are strong.

EXERCISE II.

Make a list of irregular weak verbs which have the same form for the present tense, the past tense, and the perfect participle.

EXERCISE III.

Make a list of weak verbs which have both regular and irregular forms.

EXERCISE IV.

Write the principal parts of the following verbs : —

burn,	creep,	flee,	hear,	lay,
let,	read,	set,	show,	sweep,
cost,	have,	lead,	pay,	say,
sell,	shoe,	sleep,	shut,	speed.

LESSON XXXIX.

AUXILIARY VERBS.

Compare the italicized verbs in the following sentences, and tell which express their own proper meanings and which help other verbs to express their meanings : —

1. Trees *have* roots.
2. The leaves *have* fallen.
3. It *was* an ancient mariner.
4. How cheerfully the week *was* spent!

Verbs that are used to help or complete the conjugation of other verbs, are said to be used as **auxiliaries**, and are then called **auxiliary verbs**; as, —

The rain *had* ceased.

EXERCISE I.

Point out the verbs in the following sentences, and show which are used as auxiliary verbs: —

1. The days are cold, the nights are long.
2. The sower's task is done. — BRYANT.
3. Some of the men had no muskets, and almost all were without bayonets. — HAWTHORNE.
4. Last night the moon had a golden ring.
5. I have had playmates: I have had companions. — CHARLES LAMB.
6. By fairy hands their knell is rung. — COLLINS.
7. There was a sound of revelry by night. — BYRON.
8. The shades of night were falling fast. — LONGFELLOW.
9. They know not what they do.
10. He did receive the message.
11. His face did shine as the sun.
12. I shall not look upon his like again.
13. If I will that he tarry till I come, what is that to thee? — BIBLE.
14. He will not do the work.
15. Who trusts the strength will with the burden grow.
16. The mountain and the squirrel
    Had a quarrel.

The verbs *have, do, shall, will,* and *be* are used as auxiliary verbs with the participles or infinitives of other verbs to form tense and voice. They have the following forms: —

I. — The Verb **Have.**

PRESENT TENSE.	PAST TENSE.	PERFECT PARTICIPLE.
Have.	Had.	Had.

INDICATIVE MODE.

PRESENT TENSE.		PAST TENSE.	
SINGULAR.	PLURAL.	SINGULAR.	PLURAL.
1. I have,	1. We have,	1. I had,	1. We had,
2. Thou hast,	2. You have,	2. Thou hadst,	2. You had,
3. He has.	3. They have.	3. He had.	3. They had.

SUBJUNCTIVE MODE.

PRESENT TENSE.		PAST TENSE.	
SINGULAR.	PLURAL.	SINGULAR.	PLURAL.
1. (If) I have,	1. (If) we have,	1. (If) I had,	1. (If) we had,
2. (If) thou have,	2. (If) you have,	2. (If) thou had,	2. (If) you had,
3. (If) he have.	3. (If) they have.	3. (If) he had.	3. (If) they had.

IMPERATIVE MODE.

SINGULAR.	PLURAL.
Have (thou).	Have (ye *or* you).

INFINITIVES.	PARTICIPLES.
(To) have,	*Present.* Having.
Having.	*Perfect.* Had.

The verb *have* is used as auxiliary with the perfect participle of a verb, to form the perfect tenses, each part of *have* forming the *corresponding perfect;* as, —

Present Perfect.	I have seen.
Past Perfect.	I had seen.
Future Perfect.	I shall have seen.
Perfect Infinitives.	(To) have seen ; having seen.
Perfect Participle.	Having seen.

When *have* expresses possession it is an independent verb ; as, —

Birds of the air *have* nests.

EXERCISE II.

Tell whether the verb **have** *in the following sentences is an independent verb or an auxiliary verb, giving a reason in each case :* —

1. If you have tears, prepare to shed them now.—SHAKESPEARE.

2. Have then thy wish : he whistled shrill,
And he was answered from the hill. — SCOTT.

3. Yes : he had lived to shame me from my sneer. — TAYLOR.

4. The sun had scarcely risen, when the messenger arrived.

5. Greatly begin ! though thou have time
But for a line, be that sublime. — LOWELL.

6. The things which I have seen I now can see no more.

7. The fondness for rural life among the higher classes of the English, has had a great and salutary effect upon the national character. — IRVING.

8. Of all the poets who have introduced into their works the agency of supernatural beings, Milton has succeeded best. — MACAULAY.

II. — The Verb **Do.**

The present and past tenses of the verb *do* are used as auxiliaries with the simple infinitive —

1. To express **emphasis**; as, How he *did* shake !
2. To express **negation**; as, I *did* not see it.
3. To ask a **question**; as, *Did* you hear the motion?

When *do* is used with the meaning *to perform*, it is an independent verb; as, He *did* the work quickly.

EXERCISE III.

Tell whether the verb **do** *is used as an independent or as an auxiliary verb in the following examples, and explain the use of the auxiliaries :* —

1. The evil that men do lives after them. — SHAKESPEARE.
2. You all did mark how he did shake. — SHAKESPEARE.
3. She gave me of the tree, and I did eat. — BIBLE.
4. You all do know this mantle. — SHAKESPEARE.
5. I do not like your faults. — SHAKESPEARE.
6. Accuse not nature: she hath done her part:
    Do thou but thine. — MILTON.
7. Do not dissipate your energies on trifles. — HAMILTON.
8. Most of the facts of nature, especially in the life of birds and animals, are well screened. We do not see the play because we do not look intently enough. — JOHN BURROUGHS.
9. Did ye not hear it ? — BYRON.
10. A merry heart doeth good like a medicine.

LESSON XL.

AUXILIARY VERBS. — *Continued.*

III. — Shall.

PRESENT TENSE.		PAST TENSE.	
SINGULAR.	PLURAL.	SINGULAR.	PLURAL.
1. I shall,	1. We shall,	1. I should,	1. We should,
2. Thou shalt,	2. Ye *or* you shall,	2. Thou shouldst,	2. Ye *or* you should,
3. He shall.	3. They shall.	3. He should.	3. They should.

IV. — Will.

PRESENT TENSE.		PAST TENSE.	
SINGULAR.	PLURAL.	SINGULAR.	PLURAL.
1. I will,	1. We will,	1. I would,	1. We would,
2. Thou wilt,	2. Ye *or* you will,	2. Thou wouldst,	2. Ye *or* you would,
3. He will.	3. They will.	3. He would.	3. They would.

Shall and *will* are used with the infinitive of a verb, to form the future tense. *Shall* is an auxiliary of the future in the first person, and *will* in the second and third persons; as, —

I *shall* pass the house this afternoon.
You *will* be too late.
He *will* bring the papers.

To make a promise or to express the determination of the speaker, *will* is used in the first person and *shall* in the second and third persons ; as, —

I *will* do the errand.

I *will* have my bond.

You *shall* not escape.

He *shall* receive the reward.

Shall is used in asking questions in the first person; as,—

Shall I ring the bell? (The action is dependent on the will of the person addressed.)

Should and *would*, in corresponding cases, are used in the same manner as *shall* and *will;* thus,—

I *shall* return the book, or I *should* return the book.

You *will* find the tree, or you *would* find the tree.

EXERCISE L

Explain each use of **shall** *and of* **will** *in the following sentences:—*

1. To-day the vessel shall be launched. — LONGFELLOW.

2. Take care of your spirit and conduct, and your reputation will take care of itself. — HAMILTON.

3. You will compel me then to read the will. — SHAKESPEARE.

4. Shall I descend? And will you give me leave?— SHAKESPEARE.

5. Hear me, for I will speak. — SHAKESPEARE.

6. Will you be patient? Will you stay awhile? — SHAKESPEARE.

7. If we fail, it can be no worse for us. But we shall not fail. The cause will raise up armies: the cause will create navies. — WEBSTER.

8. All that breathe will share thy destiny. — BRYANT.

9. Choose ye this day whom ye will serve.

EXERCISE II.

(1) *Copy the following sentences, filling the blanks with a form of shall or will.* (2) *State a reason for the use of each word inserted:* —

1. We —— go if it does not rain.
2. —— you have hot or cold tea?
3. The work —— probably be finished to-night.
4. Whither thou goest, I —— go; and where thou lodgest, I —— lodge. — BIBLE.
5. I —— lift up mine eyes unto the hills. — BIBLE.
6. —— I find you at home?
7. He said he —— not accept the explanation.
8. I —— be pleased to hear from you.

LESSON XLI.

AUXILIARY VERBS. — *Continued.*

V. — The Verb **Be.**

The verb **be** has the following forms: —

INDICATIVE MODE.

PRESENT TENSE.

SINGULAR.	PLURAL.
1. I am,	1. We are,
2. Thou art,	2. You are,
3. He is.	3. They are.

PAST TENSE.

SINGULAR.	PLURAL.
1. I was,	1. We were,
2. Thou wast (wert),	2. You were,
3. He was.	3. They were.

SUBJUNCTIVE MODE.

PRESENT TENSE.

SINGULAR.	PLURAL.
1. (If) I be,	1. (If) we be,
2. (If) thou be,	2. (If) you be,
3. (If) he be.	3. (If) they be.

PAST TENSE.

SINGULAR.	PLURAL.
1. (If) I were,	1. (If) we were,
2. (If) thou wert,	2. (If) you were,
3. (If) he were.	3. (If) they were.

IMPERATIVE MODE.

SINGULAR.	PLURAL.
Be (thou).	Be (ye *or* you).

INFINITIVES.	PARTICIPLES.
(To) be.	*Present.* Being.
Being.	*Perfect.* Been.

The different forms of the verb *be* are used as auxiliary —

1. With the perfect participle of a transitive verb to make the passive voice; as, —

I *am seen,*
I *was seen,*
I *shall be seen.*

I *have been seen,*
I *had been seen,*
I *shall have been seen.*

2. With the present participle of a verb, to make the **progressive form.** The progressive form represents an action as continuing or progressing ; as, —

I *am reading,*
I *was reading,*
I *shall be reading.*

I *have been reading,*
I *had been reading,*
I *shall have been reading.*

When not thus used with the participle of another verb, *be* is an independent verb. It may then —

1. Express **existence** ; as, God *is.*
2. Be used as a **copula,** connecting its subject to a word or words describing the subject ; as, Life *is* real.

EXERCISE I.

Explain the use of the verb **be** *in each of the following examples :* —

1. Life is real!   Life is earnest ! — LONGFELLOW.
2. I have been a stranger in a strange land.

3.   The harp, his sole remaining joy,
       Was carried by an orphan boy. — SCOTT.

4.   The Mayor was dumb, and the council stood
       As if they were changed into blocks of wood.

5. If money had been needed before, it was still more needed now.

6. This was accomplished in less than an hour's time.

7. The shades of night were falling fast. — LONGFELLOW.

8.
          Old Kaspar's work was done,
    And he before his cottage door
    Was sitting in the sun. — SOUTHEY.

9. While we were talking, a third messenger arrived.

10. Somewhere the birds are singing evermore.

11. O sweet and strange it seems to me, that ere this day
        is done,
    The voice, that now is speaking, may be beyond the
    sun. — TENNYSON.

12. The city was destroyed by an earthquake.

13. The great iron gateway that opened into the court-yard was locked. — IRVING.

14. Whatever is, is right. — POPE.

15. The old stage-coach is at the door.

16.
          I stood on the bridge at midnight,
          As the clocks were striking the hour.

EXERCISE II.

Copy from the sentences in this lesson (1) *all verbs that have the passive form, and* (2) *all verbs that have the progressive form, and explain the formation and the use of each.*

1. *Write five sentences, each containing the verb be used as an independent verb.*

2. *Write five sentences, each containing a verb in the passive voice.*

3. *Write five sentences, each containing a verb in the progressive form.*

—◦◦•—

LESSON XLII.

AUXILIARY VERBS. — *Continued.*

The following verbs are used with the simple infinitive to express power, permission, possibility, necessity, etc. They are sometimes called **auxiliaries of mode** : —

I. — Can.

PRESENT TENSE.		PAST TENSE.	
SINGULAR.	PLURAL.	SINGULAR.	PLURAL.
1. I can,	1. We can,	1. I could,	1. We could,
2. Thou canst,	2. Ye *or* you can,	2. Thou couldst,	2. Ye *or* you could,
3. He can.	3. They can.	3. He could.	3. They could.

Can is used to express power or ability; as : —

She *can* walk.

He *could* speak readily in three or four languages.

II. — May.

PRESENT TENSE.		PAST TENSE.	
SINGULAR.	PLURAL.	SINGULAR.	PLURAL.
1. I may,	1. We may,	1. I might,	1. We might,
2. Thou mayest,	2. Ye *or* you may,	2. Thou might-est,	2. Ye *or* you might,
3. He may.	3. They may.	3. He might.	3. They might.

May expresses permission or possibility; as, —

You *may* [*are permitted* to] enter the room.
He *may* [it *is possible* that he will] change his mind.

May is also used to express purpose, or to express a wish; as, —

Open the gate that they *may* enter.
May you be happy.

Could and *might* are sometimes used as the simple past of *can* and *may*, and sometimes in a conditional sense; as, —

I *could* hear the music.
The lights of the village *might* be seen from the bay.
He *might* go if he *could* spare the time.

III. — Must.

Must has no change of form. It expresses necessity; as, —

He *must* have rest.

IV. — Should and Would.

Should is no longer used as a simple past, but has the sense of an indefinite present or of a contingent condition; as, —

Ambition *should* be made of sterner stuff.

If I *should* begin the work, I could not finish it.

Would is sometimes a simple past, sometimes a contingent present; as, —

He *would* not speak when he had the opportunity.

He *would* not speak if he had the opportunity.

The phrases made up of the verbs *may, can, must, might, could, would,* or *should,* with an infinitive, are classed together by some grammarians, and called the potential mode; thus, —

Present Tense.	I may, can, or must go.
Present Perfect Tense.	I may have, can have, *or* must have gone.
Past Tense.	I might, could, would, *or* should go.
Past Perfect Tense.	I might have, could have, would have, *or* should have gone.

V. — Ought.

Ought is the old past tense of the verb *owe,* and expresses duty or obligation. It is used with the present infinitive to indicate present time, and with the perfect infinitive to indicate past time; as, —

Present. He ought to go.

Past. He ought to have gone.

EXERCISE I.

Tell how the verbs may, can, must, should and would are used in the following sentences : —

1. Lives of great men all remind us

    We can make our lives sublime. — LONGFELLOW.

2. For men may come and men may go,
    But I go on forever. — TENNYSON.

3. He that fights and runs away,
    May live to fight another day.

4. It may be the gulfs will wash us down :
    It may be we shall touch the Happy Isles.

5. Wealth may seek us, but wisdom must be sought.

6. It is not what a lawyer tells me I may do, but what humanity, reason, and justice tell me I ought to do. — BURKE.

7. They had been friends in youth,
    But whispering tongues can poison truth.

8. Too late! too late! ye cannot enter now. — TENNYSON.

9. How he could trot! how he could run! and then such leaps as he could take — there was not a hedge in the whole country that he could not clear. — IRVING.

10. She must weep or she will die. — TENNYSON.

11. He saw that it would be dark long before he could reach the village. — IRVING.

12. If a storm should come and awake the deep,
    What matter! I shall ride and sleep. — PROCTER.

EXERCISE II.

*Write sentences containing the verbs **may, can, must, might, could, should, and would.***

LESSON XLIII.

CONJUGATION OF THE VERB *DRIVE*.

To conjugate a verb is to give its different forms; thus,—

I.—ACTIVE VOICE.

INDICATIVE MODE.

PRESENT TENSE.

SINGULAR.	PLURAL.
1. I drive,	1. We drive,
2. Thou drivest,	2. You drive,
3. He drives.	3. They drive.

PRESENT PERFECT TENSE.

SINGULAR.	PLURAL.
1. I have driven,	1. We have driven,
2. Thou hast driven,	2. You have driven,
3. He has driven.	3. They have driven.

PAST TENSE.

SINGULAR.	PLURAL.
1. I drove,	1. We drove,
2. Thou drovest,	2. You drove,
3. He drove.	3. They drove.

PAST PERFECT TENSE.

SINGULAR.	PLURAL.
1. I had driven,	1. We had driven,
2. Thou hadst driven,	2. You had driven,
3. He had driven.	3. They had driven.

FUTURE TENSE.

SINGULAR.	PLURAL.
1. I shall drive,	1. We shall drive,
2 Thou wilt drive,	2. You will drive,
3. He will drive.	3. They will drive.

FUTURE PERFECT TENSE.

SINGULAR.	PLURAL.
1. I shall have driven,	1. We shall have driven,
2. Thou wilt have driven,	2. You will have driven,
3. He will have driven.	3. They will have driven.

SUBJUNCTIVE MODE.

PRESENT TENSE.

SINGULAR.	PLURAL.
1. (If) I drive,	1. (If) we drive,
2. (If) thou drive,	2. (If) you drive,
3. (If) he drive.	3. (If) they drive.

PAST TENSE.

SINGULAR.	PLURAL.
1. (If) I drove,	1. (If) we drove,
2. (If) thou drove,	2. (If) you drove,
3. (If) he drove.	3. (If) they drove.

IMPERATIVE MODE.

PRESENT TENSE.

SINGULAR.	PLURAL.
Drive (thou).	Drive (ye *or* you).

INFINITIVES.

PRESENT.	PERFECT.
(To) drive,	(To) have driven,
Driving.	Having driven.

PARTICIPLES.

PRESENT.	PRESENT PERFECT.
Driving.	Having driven.

II. — PASSIVE FORMS.

The passive forms of a transitive verb are made by joining its perfect participle to the different forms of the verb **be**; thus, —

INDICATIVE MODE.

Present Tense.	Present Perfect Tense.
I am driven.	I have been driven.
Past Tense.	**Past Perfect Tense.**
I was driven.	I had been driven.
Future Tense.	**Future Perfect Tense.**
I shall be driven.	I shall have been driven.

SUBJUNCTIVE MODE.

Present Tense.	Past Tense.
(If) I be driven.	(If) I were driven.

IMPERATIVE MODE.

Present Tense.

Be (thou) driven.

INFINITIVES.

Present.	Perfect.
(To) be driven,	(To) have been driven,
Being driven.	Having been driven.

PARTICIPLES.

Present.	Perfect.	Present Perfect.
Being driven.	Driven.	Having been driven.

III. — PROGRESSIVE FORMS.

The progressive forms of a verb are made by joining its present participle to the different forms of the verb **be**; thus, —

INDICATIVE MODE.

Present Tense.	Present Perfect Tense.
I am driving.	I have been driving.
Past Tense.	**Past Perfect Tense.**
I was driving.	I had been driving.
Future Tense.	**Future Perfect Tense.**
I shall be driving.	I shall have been driving,

SUBJUNCTIVE MODE.

Present Tense.	Past Tense.
(If) I be driving.	(If) I were driving.

IMPERATIVE MODE.

Present Tense.
Be (thou) driving.

INFINITIVES.

Present.	Perfect.
To (be) driving.	(To) have been driving.
	Having been driving.

PARTICIPLES.

Present.	Present Perfect.
Driving.	Having been driving.

EXERCISE I.

Write the active forms of the verb **see** *that are used with the subject* **I** *in the different modes and tenses.*

EXERCISE II.

Write the passive forms of the verb **see** *that are used with the subject* **thou** *in the different modes and tenses.*

EXERCISE III.

Write the progressive forms of the verb **write** *that are used with the subject* **he** *in the different modes and tenses.*

LESSON XLIV.

MODELS FOR PARSING VERBS, INFINITIVES, AND PARTICIPLES.

To parse a verb tell —

1. Its **conjugation** — regular or irregular.
2. Its **principal parts.**
3. Its **class** — transitive or intransitive.
4. Its **voice** — active or passive (if transitive).
5. Its **mode.**
6. Its **tense.**
7. Its **person** and **number** — when it has special forms.
8. Its **subject.**

Example I. — A flat stone *marks* the spot where the bard *is buried.*

Marks is a regular verb — mark, marked, marked. It is transitive, active voice, indicative mode, present tense, third person, singular number, agreeing with its subject *stone.*

Is buried is the passive form of the regular verb *bury* — bury, buried, buried. It is transitive, passive voice, indicative mode, present tense, third person, singular number, agreeing with its subject *bard.*

Example II. — The dew *was falling* fast.

Was falling is the progressive form of the irregular verb *fall* — fall, fell, fallen. It is intransitive, indicative mode, past tense, third person, singular number, agreeing with its subject *dew.*

Example III. — I *may do* that I *shall be* sorry for.

May is a defective verb, transitive, indicative mode, present tense, used with the subject *I.**

Do is the present infinitive of the irregular verb *do* — do, did, done. It is transitive, active voice, object of the verb *may.*

Shall be, made up of the auxiliary *shall* and the infinitive of the verb *be*, is the future tense of the verb *be*. It is irregular, — be, was, been, — intransitive, indicative mode, used with the subject *I.*

Example IV. — *Be* silent, that you may hear.

Be is an irregular verb — be, was, been, — intransitive, imperative mode, present tense, used with the subject *you* understood.

---

* Grammarians who recognize a potential mode would parse the phrase *may do,* in this example, as the potential, present, of the verb *do.*

Example V.—How he *could run!*

Could is a defective verb, transitive, indicative mode, past tense, used with the subject *he.*

Run is the present infinitive of the irregular verb *run* — run, ran, run. It is intransitive, object of the verb *could.*

Example VI.—If I should go, I *could do* your errand.

Could is a defective verb, transitive, subjunctive mode, past tense, used with the subject *I.*

Do is the present infinitive of the irregular verb *do* — do, did, done. It is transitive, active voice, object of the verb *could.*

Example VII.—The greatest curiosity of the study remains *to be mentioned;* it was a ponderous folio volume, *bound* in black leather.

To be mentioned is the present infinitive, passive, of the transitive verb *mention.* It depends on the verb *remains.*

Bound is the perfect participle, passive, of the irregular, transitive verb *bind.* It modifies the noun *volume.*

EXERCISE I.

Parse the verbs in the following sentences : —

1. Have patience with me, and I will pay thee all.
2. Now stir the fire, and close the shutters fast. — Cowper.
3. The ship is sinking beneath the tide. — Southey
4. I have been young, and now am old, yet have I not seen the righteous forsaken. — Bible.

5.   There is a tide in the affairs of men,
       Which, taken at the flood, leads on to fortune;

Omitted, all the voyage of their life
Is bound in shallows and in miseries.

6. The broad sun above laughed a pitiless .laugh.

7. The Americans were sheltered by an intervening wood.

8.   Some murmur when their sky is clear
       And wholly bright to view,
    If one small speck of dark appear
      In their great heaven of blue. — TRENCH.

9. I dreamed to-night that I did feast with Cæsar.

10. We had had no water since our daylight breakfast; our lunch on the mountain had been moistened only by the fog. — C. D. WARNER.

EXERCISE · II.

Parse the verbs, the infinitives, and the participles in the following sentences : —

1. I rose softly, opened the door suddenly, and beheld one of the most beautiful little fairy groups that a painter could imagine. — IRVING.

2. Let us enter and pass up the staircase. — HAWTHORNE.

3. In this way they expected to ruin all the merchants, and starve the poor people, by depriving them of employment. — HAWTHORNE.

4. Let me move slowly through the street. — BRYANT.

5. The country was to be defended, and to be saved, before it could be enjoyed. — WEBSTER.

6. We cannot look, however imperfectly, upon a great man without gaining something by him. — CARLYLE.

7. In an attitude imploring,
   Hands upon his bosom crossed,
Wondering, worshipping, adoring,
   Knelt the Monk in rapture lost. — LONGFELLOW.

8. The rattle of drums, beaten out of all manner of time, was heard above every other sound. — HAWTHORNE.

9. Whatever may be our fate, be assured that this declaration will stand. It may cost treasure, and it may cost blood; but it will stand, and it will richly compensate for both.

10. You may break, you may shatter the vase, if you will,
   But the scent of the roses will hang round it still.

11. For men must work, and women must weep,
   Though storms be sudden, and waters deep.

12. The burden laid upon me
   Seemed greater than I could bear.

13. Modern majesty consists in work. What a man can do is his greatest ornament, and he always consults his dignity by doing it. — CARLYLE.

14. The pine, placed nearly always among scenes disordered and desolate, brings into them all possible elements of order and precision. Lowland trees may lean to this side and that, though it is but a meadow breeze that bends them, or a bank of cowslips from which their trunks lean aslope. But let storm and avalanche do their worst, and let the pine find only a ledge of vertical precipice to cling to, it will nevertheless grow straight. — RUSKIN.

LESSON XLV.

REVIEW OF VERBS.

Define a verb. What is a transitive verb? What is an intransitive verb? Mention a word that may be a transitive verb in one sentence, and an intransitive verb in another.

What inflections have verbs? What is meant by *voice?* How many voices are there? What does each denote? How is the passive voice formed?

What is meant by mode? How many modes are there? Define, and give examples of each.

What is tense? Name the three leading tenses. Which tenses are indicated by inflection and which by the aid of other verbs?

What person-forms has the verb? What number-forms?

How do the infinitive and the participle differ from the verb? How do they differ from each other? Which part of speech is the infinitive most like? The participle? Mention four different verbal forms ending in *ing*, and state the characteristics of each.

What are the principal parts of a verb? What is a regular verb? An irregular verb? When is an irregular verb said to be strong? When weak? Are regular verbs strong or weak? Which conjugation contains the oldest verbs in the language?

What is meant by conjugating a verb?

When is a verb said to be used as an auxiliary? Mention three verbs that may be used as either independent or auxiliary verbs, and give examples of each use. What auxiliary is used in forming the passive voice? Which of the auxiliaries are tense auxiliaries? How are they used?

LESSON XLVI.

CLASSES OF ADVERBS.

Point out the adverbs in the following sentences, and tell what each expresses : —

1. Now came still evening on.
2. Ah! then and there was hurrying to and fro.
3. Days brightly came and calmly went
4. It is a very difficult task.

I. Adverbs may be classified according to their **meaning**. Thus—

1. Adverbs that show **when** or **how often** are called adverbs of **time**; as, *now, then, to-day, yesterday, early, presently, soon, always, often, once, twice, daily, again.*

2. Adverbs that show **where** are called adverbs of **place**; as, *here, there, hither, thither, hence, thence, somewhere, yonder, above, below, up, down, away, off, far.*

The word *there* is not always an adverb of place. Sometimes it is used merely to introduce a sentence, in order that the verb may be placed before its subject. When it is used to introduce a sentence in this manner, it is called an **expletive**; as, —

> *There* [expletive] was a sound of revelry by night.
> *There* [adverb of place] groups of merry children played.

3. Adverbs that show **how** are called adverbs of **manner**; as, *well, ill, badly, slowly, quickly, clearly, together, so, thus.*

4. Adverbs that show **how much** are called adverbs of **degree**; as, *very, much, little, only, almost, enough, quite, too, so, as.*

5. Adverbs that express **certainty** or **uncertainty** are called **modal adverbs**; as, *indeed, verily, possibly, perhaps.*

The words *yes* and *no* are sometimes called adverbs, but they are really abridged sentences; as, Will you go? *Yes* (= I will go).

Combinations of words used as single adverbs may be called **adverbial phrases**; as, *again and again, at last, at length, by and by, by far, in and out, in vain, now and then, out and out, through and through, up and down.*

Tell how each adverb is used in the following sentences : —

1. The guests withdrew silently.
2. The tree lies where it fell.
3. Where can rest be found?

II. Adverbs may be classified, according to use, as follows : —

1. An adverb that simply modifies another word is called a **simple adverb**; as, He walked *rapidly*.

2. An adverb that not only modifies a word, but also connects the clause of which it is a part with the remainder of the sentence, is called a **conjunctive adverb**; as, He came *when* he was called.

The most common words of this class are *when, where, whence, whither, how,* and *why*. These are also called **adverbial conjunctions**.

3. An adverb that is used to ask a question is called an **interrogative adverb**; as, *Where* did he stand?

Some adverbs admit of comparison. They are compared like adjectives; as, *soon, sooner, soonest; wisely, more wisely, most wisely; much, more, most.*

ORDER OF PARSING ADVERBS.

To parse an adverb, tell —

1. The **kind** of adverb.
2. Its **degree**, if comparative or superlative.
3. Its **construction** — what it modifies.

Example I.—He *then* touched *briefly* upon the prominent events of the Revolution.

1. *Then* is an adverb of time, modifying the verb *touched*.
2. *Briefly* is an adverb of manner, modifying the verb *touched*.

Example II.—I remember, I remember
The house *where* I was born.

Where is a conjunctive adverb, showing place. It modifies the verb *was born*, and connects the clause "where I was born" with the word *house*.

Example III.— *When* did he go?

When is an interrogative adverb of time, modifying the verb *did go*.

EXERCISE I.

Parse the verbs and the adverbs in the following sentences:—

1. A thousand hearts beat happily. — BYRON.
2. Down sunk the bell with a gurgling sound. — SOUTHEY.
3.   Then did the little maid reply,
"Seven boys and girls are we." — WORDSWORTH.

4. Defect in manners is usually the defect of fine perceptions. — EMERSON.

5.   On right, on left, above, below,
Sprung up at once the lurking foe. — SCOTT.

6.   Swiftly, swiftly flew the ship,
Yet she sailed softly too. — COLERIDGE.

7. The world is too much with us. — WORDSWORTH

8.   How often, oh, how often
           I had wished that the ebbing tide
         Would bear me away on its bosom
           O'er the ocean wild and wide. — LONGFELLOW.

EXERCISE II.

Parse the adverbs in the following sentences : —

1.   There in the twilight cold and gray,
           Lifeless, but beautiful, he lay. — LONGFELLOW.

2. And there lay the steed with his nostril all wide,
   But through it there rolled not the breath of his pride.

3. There is nothing like a primeval wood for color on a sunny day. — C. D. WARNER.

4. Why stand ye here all the day idle? — BIBLE.

5.   Oh! what a tangled web we weave,
           When first we practise to deceive. — SCOTT.

6.   O Solitude! where are the charms
             That sages have seen in thy face? — COWPER.

7. O, why should the spirit of mortal be proud? — KNOX.

8. The rain is falling where they lie. — BRYANT.

ADJECTIVE OR ADVERB.

Tell whether the italicized words in the following sentences are adjectives or adverbs, giving a reason in each case : —

1. She looks *cold.*

2. She looked *coldly* on the project.

3. The apple feels *hard.*
4. He works *hard.*

An adjective is used when the quality or condition of the subject is given, and an adverb, when the manner of the action is described; as, —

The child seems *happy.*
He lived *happily.*

Some adverbs are identical in form with adjectives; as, *much, little, far, ill, hard, loud, soft, fast.*

EXERCISE III.

Parse the adverbs and the adjectives in the following sentences : —

1. He lives long that lives well.
2. Still waters run deep.
3. Welcome her, all things youthful and sweet!
4. Then they praised him soft and low.
5. He drank of the water so cool and clear. — SOUTHEY.
6. How fast the flitting figures come! — BRYANT.
7. The shades of night were falling fast. — LONGFELLOW.
8. The door in the mountain-side shut fast.
9. A wondrous portal opened wide. — BROWNING.
10. The tumult grew louder. — HAWTHORNE.
11. Louder still the minstrels blew.

12.   Colder and louder blew the wind,
        A gale from the Northeast. — LONGFELLOW.

EXERCISE IV.

What is an adverb? How are adverbs classified with respect to meaning? Give an example of each class. How are they classified with respect to use? State the two offices of a conjunctive adverb. Give an example of an interrogative adverb. Mention five adverbs that admit of comparison, and give the comparison of each. In what way are adjectives and adverbs alike? How do they differ?

LESSON XLVII.

PREPOSITIONS.

Tell what the following prepositions connect, and what relations they express : —

1. He 'stood *on* the bridge.
2. 'Twas the night *before* Christmas.
3. The tree was struck *by* lightning.
4. He died *for* his country.
5. The eyes *of* the sleepers waxed deadly and chill.

Prepositions express such a variety of relations that they cannot be easily classified according to meaning. The most common relations expressed by prepositions are —

1. **Place** or **direction**; as, *At* home; *towards* the bridge; *below* the falls.
2. **Time**; as, *After* breakfast; *till* noon; *since* morning.
3. **Agency, instrumentality, or means**; as, Killed *by* frost; cut *with* a hatchet; lost *through* carelessness.

4. **Cause,** or **purpose**; as, Thankful *for* good health; He votes *from* principle.

5. **Possession**; as, The voice *of* the speaker; the beauty *of* the rose; the blade *of* the knife.

6. **Definition**; as, The virtue *of* temperance; the city *of* Rome.

7. **Object**; as, The fear *of* death; the hope *of* reward.

Many other relations are implied, such as *reference*, expressed by *about; association*, by *with; separation*, by *from; opposition*, by *against; substitution*, by *for;* etc.

Certain phrases are used with the force of single prepositions. They are called compound prepositions; as, *according to, in place of, in regard to, instead of, out of, on account of.*

Order of Parsing Prepositions.

To parse a preposition, —

1. Name the part of speech.
2. Tell with what word it connects its object.
3. State the relation shown.

Example. — He goes *on* Sunday *to* the church. — Longfellow.

1. *On* is a preposition, connecting the noun *Sunday* with the verb *goes*, and showing the relation of time.

2. *To* is a preposition, connecting the noun *church* with the verb *goes*, and showing the relation of place.

EXERCISE I.

Parse the prepositions in the following sentences: —

1. At midnight, however, I was aroused by the tramp of horses' hoofs in the yard.

2. Great turtles came up out of the water, and crawled along on a sandy place. — M. Thompson.

3. The scheme failed for want of support.

4.
    The Love that leads the willing spheres
    Along the unending track of years
    And watches o'er the sparrow's nest,
    Shall brood above thy winter rest. — Bryant.

5.
    By fairy hands their knell is rung;
    By forms unseen their dirge is sung. — Collins.

6.
        With my cross-bow
    I shot the Albatross. — Coleridge.

7. The little bird sits at his door in the sun. — Lowell.

EXERCISE II.

Parse the prepositions and the adverbs in the following: —

On the cross-beam under the Old South bell
The nest of a pigeon is builded well.
In summer and winter that bird is there,
Out and in with the morning air;
I love to see him track the street,
With his wary eye and active feet;
And I often watch him as he springs,
Circling the steeple with easy wings,
Till across the dial his shade has passed,
And the belfry edge is gained at last. — N. P. Willis.

LESSON XLVIII.

CLASSES OF CONJUNCTIONS.

I.—CO-ORDINATING CONJUNCTIONS.

Find in the following examples conjunctions that connect sentences, or words, phrases, and clauses of like kind, or having the same relation to the rest of the sentence : —

1. Art is long, and time is fleeting.

2. Games and carols closed the day.

3. The house was silent and deserted.

4. You see where Warren fell, and where other patriots fell with him.

Words, phrases, and clauses of like kind, or standing in the same relation to the rest of the sentence, are said to have the same construction or to be of equal rank. Conjunctions that connect sentences, or parts of sentences of equal rank, are called **co-ordinating conjunctions.** They may connect —

1. Two independent sentences ; as, *Be diligent, and you will succeed.*

2. Two words in the same construction ; as, The minstrel was *infirm and old.*

3. Two phrases in the same construction ; as, They are alike *in voice and in manner.*

4. Two dependent clauses in the same construction ; as, No one could tell *whence they came or whither they went.*

Co-ordinating conjunctions are divided into the following classes : —

1. **Copulative,** those that join similar parts ; as, *and, also, besides, likewise, moreover.*

2. **Adversative,** those that join parts opposed in meaning ; as, *but, yet, however, still, nevertheless, notwithstanding.*

3. **Alternative,** those that imply a choice between two ; as, *either —or, neither—nor, whether—or.*

4. **Causal,** those that express cause or consequence ; as, *for, therefore, hence, consequently.*

Conjunctions used in pairs are called **correlatives** ; as, *both— and, either—or, neither—nor, not—but, not only—but.*

II.—SUBORDINATING CONJUNCTIONS.

Mention the dependent clause in each of the following sentences, state its use, and tell how it is joined to the principal clauses.

> 1. I would grant your request if I could.
> 2. He came, because he was needed.
> 3. Be silent, that you may hear.

Conjunctions that connect a dependent or subordinate clause to a principal clause are called **subordinating conjunctions.** They denote —

1. **Time** ; as, *after, before, ere, since, till, when, while, as.*
2. **Place** ; as, *where, whence.*
3. **Manner and comparison** ; as, *than, as.*
4. **Cause or reason** ; as, *because, since, as, that, whereas.*
5. **End or purpose** ; as, *that, lest.*
6. **Condition** ; as, *if, unless, except.*
7. **Concession** ; as, *though, although.*

Certain phrases performing the office of conjunctions may be called **compound conjunctions** ; as, *but also, as well as, as if, as though.*

ORDER OF PARSING CONJUNCTIONS.

To parse a conjunction, tell —

1. **Its class** — co-ordinating or subordinating.
2. **Its use** — state what it connects.

Example I. — Hear me for my cause, *and* be silent, *that* you may hear.

1. *And* is a co-ordinating conjunction, connecting the two independent members, "Hear me for my cause," and "be silent, that you may hear."

2. *That* is a subordinating conjunction, connecting the subordinate clause, "you may hear," to the principal clause, "be silent."

Example II. — Is the night chilly *and* dark?

1. *And* is a co-ordinating conjunction, connecting the two adjectives *chilly* and *dark*.

EXERCISE I.

Parse the conjunctions in the following sentences, and state the relation between the connected terms : —

1. My hair is gray, but not with years,
  　　Nor grew it white
  　　In a single night,
  As men's have grown from sudden fears:
  My limbs are bowed, though not with toil,
  　But rusted with a vile repose,
  For they have been a dungeon's spoil,
  　And mine has been the fate of those
  To whom the goodly earth and air
  Are banned, and barred, — forbidden fare. — BYRON.

2. Here rests his head upon the lap of earth,
  A youth to fortune and to fame unknown. — GRAY.

3. They deserved respect; for they were good men as well as brave. — HAWTHORNE.

4.   On either side the river lie
      Long fields of barley and of rye. — TENNYSON.

5. Neither a borrower nor a lender be. — SHAKESPEARE.

6. As Cæsar loved me, I weep for him; as he was fortunate, I rejoice at it; as he was valiant, I honor him: but, as he was ambitious, I slew him. — SHAKESPEARE.

7. The test of a people is not in its occupations, but in its heroes. — T. W. HIGGINSON.

8.   Then they praised him, soft and low,
         Called him worthy to be loved,
      Truest friend and noblest foe;
         Yet she neither spoke nor moved. — TENNYSON.

9. One whole month elapsed before I knew the fate of the cargo.

10. The works of Milton cannot be comprehended or enjoyed, unless the mind of the reader co-operate with that of the writer. He does not paint a finished picture, or play for a mere passive listener. He sketches, and leaves others to fill up the outline. He strikes the key-note, and expects his hearer to make out the melody. — MACAULAY.

EXERCISE II.

Name the two leading classes of conjunctions. What is a co-ordinating conjunction? What is meant by words, phrases, or clauses of equal rank? Illustrate. Tell how co-ordinating conjunctions are classified, and give examples of each class.

What is a subordinating conjunction? Mention some of the different relations denoted by subordinating conjunctions, and give illustrations.

What are correlative conjunctions? Give examples.

Mention phrases that are used as conjunctions.

LESSON XLIX.

INTERJECTIONS.

Since interjections are not grammatically related to the other words in a sentence, the parsing of an interjection consists in simply naming the part of speech.

EXERCISE.

Mention the interjections in the following sentences, and tell what feeling each expresses: —

1.   Ah! what would the world be to us
      If the children were no more? — LONGFELLOW.

2. Hark! let me listen for the swell of the surf.

3. Ah! what a weary race my feet have run. — WARTON.

4. Oh! wherefore come ye forth, in triumph from the North? — MACAULAY.

5. Alas! I have nor hope nor health. — SHELLEY.

6. And, lo! from far, as on they pressed, there came a glittering band. — HEMANS

7. Hark! hark! the lark at heaven's gate sings.

8. Ha! laugh'st thou, Lochiel, my vision to scorn?

9.   For, lo! the blazing, rocking roof
      Down, down in thunder falls! — HORACE SMITH.

10.   Heigh ho! daisies and buttercups,
      Fair yellow daffodils, stately and tall.

11.   O joy! that in our embers
      Is something that doth live. — WORDSWORTH.

SUMMARY.

INFLECTION.

Inflection is the alteration in the form of a word, to express a change of meaning or of relation.

The parts of speech that are inflected are the noun, the pronoun, the adjective, the verb, and the adverb.

Nouns and pronouns are inflected for gender, number, and case. The inflection of a noun or a pronoun is called its *declension.*

Verbs are inflected for voice, mode, tense, person, and number. The inflection of a verb is called its *conjugation.*

Some adjectives and a few adverbs are inflected for degree. This inflection is called *comparison.*

Prepositions, conjunctions, and interjections are not inflected.

PART THIRD.

RELATIONS OF WORDS—SYNTAX.

SYNTAX treats of the grammatical relations of words in sentences. The relation that any part of speech bears to other parts of speech in the same sentence is called its **construction.**

———◦○✕○◦———

LESSON L.

CONSTRUCTIONS OF THE NOUN.

The most common constructions of the noun have already been given. The noun may be used —

1. As the **subject of a verb**; as, —

The sun shines.

The subject of a verb is in the **nominative case.** This is called the **subject nominative.**

2. As a **predicate nominative.** A noun that completes the meaning of an intransitive verb, and refers to the same person or thing as the subject of the verb, is said to be in the **nominative case** after the verb. It completes the predicate, and is called a **predicate noun** or a **predicate nominative.** The verbs *be, become, appear, look, seem,* etc., and the passive forms of a few transitive verbs are followed by a predicate nominative; as, —

Webster was a statesman.

Man became a living *soul.*

He was elected *senator.*

3. As an objective predicate; as, —

They made him *secretary.*

In this sentence *him* is the direct object of the verb, and *secretary* completes the meaning of the verb *make* and shows what they made him.   A noun that completes the meaning of a transitive verb and describes its object is called an **objective predicate.** The verbs *make, appoint, elect, call, choose,* and others of similar meaning, are followed by the **objective predicate.**

When these verbs are used in the passive voice, they are followed by the **predicate nominative;** as, —

He will be made *secretary.*

4. **In apposition.**   A noun added to a noun or a pronoun, to explain or describe its meaning, is called an **appositive,** or is said to be in **apposition** with the first noun or pronoun.   Two words in apposition are in the same case; as, —

Motley, the *historian,* was an American.   (Nominative case.)

We met your brother, the *general.*   (Objective case.)

5. **In the nominative absolute.**   A noun used absolutely with a participle, its case not depending upon any other word, is said to be in the **nominative case absolute;** as, —

The *train* being late, they returned to the hotel.

6. **In address.**   When a noun is used in addressing a person or a thing, it is said to be in the nominative case of **address;** as, —

Friends, are you convinced?

Ring, happy *bells,* across the snow.

7. As a **possessive** modifying another noun; as,—

We sat by the *fisher's* cottage.

The noun denoting the thing possessed is sometimes omitted; as, He called at your mother's [*house*].

8. As the **object of a transitive verb** (or of its participles or infinitives); as, —

The boy waved a *flag*.
The horse, hearing the *cars*, stopped.
'Tis sweet to hear the merry *lark*.

9. As the **object of a preposition**; as,—

We spoke not a word of *sorrow*.

10. As an **indirect object** to show **to** or **for** whom or what something is done; as,—

He gave the *man* a coat (He gave a coat *to* the man).

In the first form, the noun *coat* is the direct object of the verb *gave*, and the noun *man* the indirect object.

She bought the *bird* a cage (She bought a cage *for* the bird).

In the first form, the noun *cage* is the direct object of the verb *bought*, and the noun *bird* is the indirect object.

As these examples show, the *indirect* object alone is used when the noun stands next the verb, the preposition when the noun is separated from the verb.

11. As an **adverbial limitation** to modify a verb, an adjective, or an adverb. When nouns expressing *time, distance, weight, value,* etc., are used like adverbs, they are called **adverbial objects**, or are said to be in the **objective case, adverbially**; as, —

He *held* the office three *years*.
The walk is three *feet wide*.
Do not remain a *moment longer*.

EXERCISE L.

Name the case, and give the construction of each noun in the following sentences : —

1. Every man's task is his life-preserver. — EMERSON.

2. He took great pains to give us all the information we needed. — HOLMES.

3.   Then give him, for a soldier meet,
     A soldier's cloak for winding-sheet. — SCOTT.

4. I am monarch of all I survey. — COWPER.

5.   Our fortress is the good greenwood,
     Our tent the cypress-tree. — BRYANT.

6. They made me queen of the May. — TENNYSON.

7. The colonists were now no longer freemen; they were entirely dependent on the king's pleasure. — HAWTHORNE.

8.   The harp, his sole remaining joy,
     Was carried by an orphan boy. — SCOTT.

9. Brethren, the sower's task is done. — BRYANT.

10.   Yet fair as thou art, thou shunnest to glide,
      Beautiful stream ! by the village side. — BRYANT.

11. The supper being over, the strangers requested to be shown to their place of repose. — HAWTHORNE.

12. An ancient clock, that important article of cottage furniture, ticked on the opposite side of the room. — IRVING.

13. Good friends, sweet friends, let me not stir you up to such a sudden flood of mutiny. — SHAKESPEARE.

14. We have no bird whose song will match the nightingale's in compass, none whose note is so rich as that of the European blackbird; but for mere rapture I have never heard the bobolink's rival. — LOWELL.

EXERCISE II.

1. *Write sentences illustrating five different constructions of a noun in the nominative case.*

2. *Write sentences illustrating six different constructions of a noun in the objective case.*

LESSON LI.

CONSTRUCTIONS OF THE PRONOUN.

I. — AGREEMENT WITH ANTECEDENT.

What determines the person, number, and gender of the italicized pronouns in the following sentences? —

1. The host moved about among *his* guests.
2. Here is the lady *that* rang the bell.
3. Uneasy lies the head *that* wears a crown.

A pronoun must agree in person, number, and gender with its antecedent.

The antecedent of a relative pronoun is sometimes omitted; as, [*He*] Who breaks, pays.

The relative pronoun is sometimes omitted; as, Observe the language well in all [*that*] you write.

It is sometimes used indefinitely without an antecedent, as the subject or as the object of a verb; as, *It* rains. Come and trip *it* as you go. This is often called the **impersonal** use.

It is often used as the subject of a verb which is followed by the real subject; as, *It* is impossible *to hear*.

EXERCISE L

Give the antecedent, and the person, number, and gender of each pronoun in the following sentences: —

1. The evil that men do lives after them.
2. Not a boy in the class knew his lesson.

3. And the women are weeping and wringing their hands
   For those who will never come home to the town.

4. He that is giddy thinks that the world turns round.
5. What is that sound which now bursts on his ear?
6. After the dinner-table was removed, the hall was given up to the younger members of the family, who made its old walls ring with their merriment as they played at romping games. — IRVING.

7.   I thrice presented him a kingly crown,
       Which he did thrice refuse. — SHAKESPEARE.

8.   Thou art Freedom's now, and Fame's,
       One of the few, the immortal names,
       That were not born to die. — HALLECK.

II. — CASE-RELATIONS.

The case-relations of the pronoun are the same as those of the noun.

EXERCISE I.

Explain the use of each italicized case-form in the following sentences : —

1. If *I* were *he,* I should not go.
2. It must have been *she whom* you saw.
3. To *whom* did *he* refer?
4. Do *you* know *who* I am?
5. *Who* do *you* think will be chosen?
6. *Whom* did he call?
7. *Whom* do you wish to see?
8. *Who* is it that you wish to see?
9. Could it have been *they that* called?
10. I am *he whom* you seek.
11. Is it *I* that you mean?
12. Between you and *me,* I do not care how the matter ends.

EXERCISE II.

Mention the case, and state the construction of each italicized pronoun in the following sentences : —

1. The great man is *he who* does not lose his child's heart.
2. I know not what course *others* may take; but, as for me, give *me* liberty or give *me* death! — PATRICK HENRY.
3. *It* is *I;* be not afraid. — BIBLE.
4. *What* do *we* give to *our* beloved? — E. B. BROWNING.

5.   *What* in *me* is dark,
Illumine; *what* is low, raise and support. — Milton.

6. *Who*, of all *that* address the public ear, whether in church, or court-house, or hall of state, has such an attentive audience as the town-crier? — Hawthorne.

7. *We all* do fade as a leaf. — Bible.

8. *He* is the freeman *whom* the truth makes free.

9.   Breathes there the man with soul so dead
Who never to *himself* hath said,
This is my own, my native land? — Scott.

10.   "Hadst *thou* stayed I must have fled!"
This is *what* the vision said. — Longfellow.

LESSON LII.

CONSTRUCTIONS OF THE ADJECTIVE.

Which adjectives in the following sentences modify nouns directly, and which modify a noun or a pronoun through the verb? —

1. A soft answer turneth away wrath.
2. Ring out, wild bells.
3. The sky is clear.
4. He painted the house white.
5. Her beauty made me glad.

I. An adjective that modifies a noun or a pronoun directly is said to be used **attributively**; as, —

Drowsy tinklings lull the *distant* fold.

II. An adjective loosely attached to its noun is said to be used **appositively**; as, —

No misfortune, *public* or *private*, could oppress him.

III. An adjective that completes the predicate, and shows what is asserted of the subject of the verb, or describes the object of the verb, is called a **predicate adjective,** or is said to be used **predicatively**; as, —

Snow is *white*.
They set the prisoner *free*.

In poetry an adjective is sometimes used for an adverb; as, —

Silent rows the gondolier.

EXERCISE I.

Tell how each adjective is used in the following sentences: —

1. The lamps shone o'er fair women and brave men.

2. Is it where the feathery palm-trees rise,
   And the date grows ripe under sunny skies?
   Or 'midst the green islands of glittering seas,
   Where fragrant forests perfume the breeze?

3. The fields were green, and the sky was blue. — SOUTHEY.

4. The sea is mighty, but a mightier sways
   His restless billows. — BRYANT.

5. He wrapped her warm in his seaman's coat.
6. My keepers grew compassionate. — BYRON.
7. Besides, our losses have made us thrifty. — BROWNING.

8. Heigh-ho! daisies and buttercups,
   Fair yellow daffodils, stately and tall!
When the wind wakes, how they rock in the grasses,
   And dance with the cuckoo-buds, slender and small!

EXERCISE II.

1. *Write four sentences containing adjectives used attributively.*

2. *Write three sentences containing adjectives used predicatively, with intransitive verbs.*

3. *Write three sentences containing adjectives used predicatively, with transitive verbs.*

LESSON LIII.

THE VERB.

AGREEMENT WITH SUBJECT.

What determines the person and number forms of the italicized verbs in the following sentences? —

1. The stream *flows* swiftly.
2. Thou *art* the man.
3. John and Henry *are* absent.
4. John or Henry *is* absent.
5. The committee *has* been appointed.

When the form of the subject determines the form of the verb, a verb is said to **agree** with its subject in person and number; as,—

I *see;* thou *seest;* he *sees.*

Two or more singular subjects connected by *and* **require a plural verb;** as, —

Time and *tide* wait for no man.

If the subjects refer to the same person or thing, the verb must be singular; as, The soldier and statesman *has* passed away.

When the subjects are preceded by *each, every,* or *no,* they refer to things considered separately, and require a singular verb; as, Each day and each hour brings its own duties.

Two or more singular subjects connected by *or* **or** *nor* **require a singular verb;** as, —

He or she *was* in the wrong.

A collective noun requires a verb in the singular when it denotes the collection as a whole, and a verb in the plural, when it denotes the individuals in the collection separately; as, —

The congregation *was* dismissed.
The whole congregation *were* in tears.

EXERCISE I.

State the person and the number of each italicized verb in the following sentence, and tell why these forms are used: —

1. The difficulties *were* all over now, and everything *was* settled.

2. A little fire *is* quickly trodden out.

3. Delicacy and brilliancy *characterize* nearly all the California flowers.

4. The derivation of these words *is* uncertain.

5. It is an ill wind that *blows* nobody good.

6. Neither the secretary nor the treasurer *was* present.

7. The army is *needed* for the defence of the country.

8. How *does* such a loose pile of sticks maintain its place during a heavy wind?

9. A hundred eager fancies and busy hopes *keep* him awake.

10. The council *were* divided in their opinions.

11. Slow and sure *comes* up the golden year.

12. Either ability or inclination *was* wanting.

13. Let us hold fast the great truth that the people *are* responsible.

14. A word or an epithet *paints* a whole scene.

15. The saint, the father, and the husband *prays.* — BURNS.

16. Seasons *return*, but not to me *returns*
Day, or the sweet approach of even or morn. — MILTON.

EXERCISE II.

1. *Write three sentences in each of which the verb has two or more singular subjects connected by* **and**.

2. *Write three sentences in each of which the verb has two or more singular subjects connected by* **or** *or* **nor**.

3. *Write two sentences in each of which the subject is a collective noun denoting the collection as a whole.*

4. *Write two sentences in each of which the subject is a collective noun denoting the individuals in the collection separately.*

LESSON LIV.

CONSTRUCTIONS OF INFINITIVES.

The chief constructions of the infinitives, including those already given, are the following : —

I. The simple infinitive, without **to**, is used after the verbs *may, can, must, dare*, etc., as, —

> Men must *work*.

II. Both the infinitive with **to** and the participial infinitive may be used, like a noun —

1. As the subject of a verb; as, —

> *To see* is to believe.
> *Seeing* is believing.

2. As a predicate nominative; as, —

> To hesitate is *to fail*.
> Begging is not *serving*.

3. As the object of a verb; as, —

> We purpose *to call* a meeting.
> We purpose *calling* a meeting.

4. As the object of a preposition.

> She was about *to speak*.
> On *reaching* the door, he paused.

III. The infinitive with **to** is used —

1. To modify a noun, an adjective, or an adverb; as, —

> There is a time *to weep*.

She is eager *to go*.

He is old enough *to know* better.

2. To express **purpose**, consequence, etc.; as, —

He came *to assist* his comrades.

3. **Elliptically** or **absolutely**; as, —

He was petrified, so *to speak*.

To tell the truth, I do not believe it.

IV. The infinitive, usually with **to**, is used with a noun or a pronoun as the **object** of a **verb**; as, —

He maketh *wars to cease*.

I asked *him to sing*.

In this construction, the noun or pronoun which is used with the infinitive as the object of the verb is called the subject of the infinitive. The subject of an infinitive is in the objective case.

A few simple verbs, such as *let, hear, see*, etc., take in this construction the simple infinitive; as, Let me *go;* I saw him *fall*.

V. The participial infinitive, like the noun, **takes a possessive noun** or **pronoun**; as, —

Much depends on *Robert's receiving* the message.

His coming was not unexpected.

EXERCISE I.

Point out the infinitives in the following sentences, and state the construction of each: —

1. For him, to hear is to obey. ·
2. A sower went forth to sow.
3. He taught her to see new beauties in nature. —IRVING.

4. I come not, friends, to steal away your hearts.

5. The sun is just about to set. — TENNYSON.

6.   And many a holy text around she strews
     That teach the rustic moralist to die. — GRAY.

7.   She heard the birds sing, she
     Saw the sun shine. — LONGFELLOW.

8. After tarrying a few days in the bay, our voyagers weighed anchor, to explore a mighty river which emptied into the bay. — IRVING.

9. And fools who came to scoff remained to pray.

10. I did send to you for gold to pay my legions. — SHAKESPEARE.

11. Hast thou a charm to stay the morning star? — COLERIDGE.

12. Upon the landlord's leaving the room, I could not avoid expressing my concern for the stranger. — GOLDSMITH.

13.   To live in hearts we leave behind
     Is not to die. — CAMPBELL.

14. Beyond that I seek not to penetrate the veil. — WEBSTER.

EXERCISE II.

I. *Write three sentences containing the simple infinitive without* **to.**

II. *Write four sentences containing infinitives used like nouns.*

III. *Write two sentences containing infinitives used like adjectives.*

IV. *Write three sentences containing infinitives used like adverbs.*

LESSON LV.

CONSTRUCTIONS OF PARTICIPLES.

Participles modify nouns or pronouns. They may be used —

I. **Attributively;** as, —

The *rising* sun hides the stars.

II. **Appositively,** usually equivalent to an implied clause; as, —

Truth, *crushed* to earth, shall rise again.

III. **Predicatively;** as, —

Here it runs *sparkling*.
He kept us *waiting*.

IV. **Absolutely;** as, —

The service *having closed*, we left the church.

EXERCISE I.

Parse the participles and the infinitives in the following sentences : —

1. As we stood waiting on the platform, a telegraphic message was handed in silence to my companion. — HOLMES.

2. An uprooted tree came drifting along the current, and became entangled among the rocks.

3. "Ah!" cried he, drawing back in surprise.

4. The turban folded about his head
Was daintily wrought of the palm-leaf braid.

5. At each corner of the building is an octagon tower, surmounted by a gilt ball and weathercock. — IRVING.

6. All the stories of ghosts and goblins that he had heard in the afternoon, now came crowding upon his recollection.

7. I saw you sitting in the house, and I no longer there.

8. The snow fell hissing in the brine,
And the billows frothed like yeast. — LONGFELLOW.

9. Upon his advancing toward me with a whisper, I expected to hear some secret piece of news. — ADDISON.

10. A word fitly spoken is like apples of gold in pictures of silver. — BIBLE.

11. His father being at the warehouse, did not yet know of the accident. — GEORGE ELIOT.

12. The wind having failed at sunset, the crew set to work with a will.

13. Here is a good place to test the qualities of a book as an out-door companion.

14. There is not wind enough to twirl
The one red leaf, the last of its clan,
That dances as often as dance it can,
Hanging so light, and hanging so high,
On the topmost twig that looks up at the sky. — COLERIDGE.

15. The talent of success is nothing more than doing what you can do, well. — LONGFELLOW.

16. To reverse the rod, to spell the charm backward, to break the ties which bound a stupefied people to the seat of enchantment, was the noble aim of Milton. — MACAULAY.

SUMMARY.

RULES OF SYNTAX.

1. The subject of a finite verb is in the nominative case.

2. The verbs *be, become, appear, look, seem,* etc., and the passive forms of the transitive verbs *make, appoint,* etc., take the same case after them as before them.

3. A noun added to another noun to explain or describe its meaning is in the same case by apposition.

4. A noun or a pronoun used absolutely with a participle is in the nominative case absolute.

5. A noun used in addressing a person or a thing, is in the nominative case of address.

6. A noun or a pronoun used, like an adjective, to modify another noun, is in the possessive case.

7. Transitive verbs in the active voice, and their participles and infinitives, take nouns and pronouns in the objective case.

8. Verbs like *give, buy, teach,* etc., take two objects — the one direct, the other indirect.

9. The verbs *make, appoint, choose,* etc., are followed in the active voice by a direct object and an objective predicate.

10. Prepositions are followed by nouns or pronouns in the objective case.

11. Nouns used adverbially are in the objective case.

12. The subject of an infinitive is in the objective case.

13. A pronoun must agree in person, number, and gender with its antecedent.

14. An adjective modifies a noun or a pronoun.

15. A verb must agree with its subject in person and in number.

16. An adverb modifies a verb, an adjective, or another adverb.

LESSON LVI.

DIFFERENT USES OF THE SAME WORD.

Give a reason for the classification of each italicized word in the following examples : —

All :

1. *All* men are mortal. (Adjective.)
2. *All* joined in the song. (Adjective Pronoun.)
3. My *all* is lost. (Noun.)
4. I am *all* alone. (Adverb.)

As :

1. He wrote *as* (Adverb of Degree) well *as* (Conjunctive Adverb) he could.
2. *As* he was ambitious, I slew him. (Conjunction.)
3. The days of man are but *as* grass [is]. (Conjunction.)
4. We are such stuff *as* dreams are made of. (Relative Pronoun.)

Before :

1. He stood *before* me. (Preposition.)
2. Look *before* you leap. (Conjunction.)
3. She had not entered this hall *before*. (Adverb.)

Both :

1. Stretch out *both* thy hands. (Adjective.)
2. She *both* laughed and cried. (Conjunction.)

But :

1. Fools admire, *but* men of sense approve. (Conjunction)
2. Nought is heard *but* [except] the lashing waves. (Preposition.)

3. Man wants *but* little here below. (Adverb.)

4.   There is no fireside, howsoe'er defended,
But has one vacant chair. (Relative Pronoun.)

Else :

1. Anybody *else* would consent. (Adjective.)
2. Where *else* could he go? (Adverb.)
3. I have no tears, *else* would I weep for thee. (Conjunction.)

Enough :

1. *Enough* is as good as a feast. (Noun.)
2. They have books *enough.* (Adjective.)
3. He has worked long *enough.* (Adverb.)

Except :

1. No one heard the alarm *except* me. (Preposition.)
2. I will not let thee go, *except* thou bless me. (Conjunction.)

For :

1. We shall wait *for* the boat. (Preposition.)
2. I called, *for* I was wild with fear. (Conjunction.)

However :

1. *However* busy he may be, he will aid you. (Adverb.)
2. These conditions, *however*, he could not accept. (Conjunction.)

Like :

1. This box is *like* yours. (Adjective.)
2. He ran *like* a deer. (Adverb.)
3. I *like* to read. (Verb.)

Since:

1. I have not thought of the matter *since*. (Adverb.)
2. We have not heard from him *since* morning. (Preposition.)
3. *Since* the books are here, we will use them. (Conjunction.)

So:

1. *So* ended the conflict. (Adverb.)
2. The library was closed, *so* we returned home. (Conjunction.)

That:

1. *That* book is lost. (Adjective.)
2. *That* is the cause of the trouble. (Adjective Pronoun.)
3. Here is the man *that* gave the order. (Relative Pronoun.)
4. I know *that* the work will be done. (Conjunction.)

The:

1. *The* way was long. (Adjective.)
2. *The* more, *the* merrier. (Adverb of Degree.)

LESSON LVII.

SELECTIONS FOR STUDY.

Parse the italicized words in the following exercises, giving a full explanation of the different constructions:—

EXERCISE I.

Whoever *has made* a voyage *up* the Hudson, *must remember* the Kaatskill Mountains. *They* are a dismembered *branch* of the great *Appalachian family*, and *are seen away* to the west of the river, *swelling up* to a noble height, *and lording it over* the surrounding *country*. Every *change* of season, *every* change of *weather, indeed,* every *hour* of the day, *produces some* change in the magical *hues and* shapes of *these mountains; and* they *are regarded* by *all* the good *wives, far and near, as* perfect *barometers*. *When* the weather is *fair* and *settled,* they *are clothed* in *blue* and *purple,* and *print* their bold *outlines on* the clear evening sky; *but sometimes, when* the *rest* of the *landscape is cloudless,* they *will gather* a *hood* of gray vapors *about* their summits, *which in* the last rays *of* the *setting* sun, *will glow* and *light up like* a *crown* of *glory.* — WASHINGTON IRVING.

EXERCISE II.

"Have, then, thy wish!" He whistled *shrill,*
And he *was answered from* the hill;
Wild as the *scream of* the curlew,
From crag *to* crag the signal *flew.*
Instant, through copse *and* heath, *arose*
Bonnets *and* spears *and* bended bows;
On *right,* on *left, above, below,*
Sprung up at once the *lurking foe;*
From shingles gray *their* lances *start,*
The bracken *bush* sends *forth* the *dart,*
The rushes *and* the willow-wand
Are bristling into axe *and* brand,
And every tuft of broom *gives life*
To plaided *warrior armed* for strife. — SIR WALTER SCOTT.

EXERCISE III.

All the *inhabitants* of the little village are busy. *One is clearing* a *spot* on the verge *of* the forest *for* his homestead; *another* is hewing the trunk of a *fallen pine-tree, in order to build himself* a *dwelling;* a third *is hoeing* in his field of Indian corn. *Here comes* a huntsman *out of* the woods, *dragging* a bear *which* he has shot, *and shouting* to the neighbors *to lend him* a *hand. There goes* a *man* to the *sea-shore, with* a spade *and* a bucket, *to dig* a mess of clams, *which* were a principal *article* of food with the first settlers. *Scattered here* and *there* are two *or* three dusky *figures, clad* in mantles *of* fur, with ornaments of bone *hanging* from *their* ears, and the feathers of *wild* birds in their *coal-black* hair. They have *belts* of shell-work *slung across* their shoulders, and are *armed* with bows and arrows and *flint-headed* spears. *These* are an Indian *sagamore* and his attendants, *who* have come *to gaze* at the labors of the white men. *And now rises* a *cry that* a *pack* of wolves *have seized* a young calf in the pasture; and every man *snatches up* his gun or pike and *runs* in chase of the *marauding* beasts. — NATHANIEL HAWTHORNE.

PART FOURTH.

STRUCTURE AND ANALYSIS OF SENTENCES.

———∘o:❀:o∘———

LESSON LVIII.

STRUCTURE OF THE SENTENCE.

A **sentence** is the expression of a complete thought in words.

A sentence consists of two parts: the part of a sentence that shows what is spoken of is called the **subject**; the part that tells something about the thing spoken of is called the **predicate**.

The subject of a sentence consists of a noun (or of a word or words equivalent to a noun), alone or with additional words called **adjuncts** or **modifiers**. The subject noun without modifiers is called the **grammatical, or bare, subject**; as, *Birds* fly.

The grammatical subject with its modifiers is called the **logical, or complete, subject**; as, —

> *The inhabitants of the little village* are busy.

The predicate of a sentence is a verb, alone or with adjuncts. The predicate verb without adjuncts is called the **grammatical, or bare, predicate**; as, The sun *rose*.

Some verbs do not form a predicate alone. A verb that requires an additional word to complete the predicate is called a verb of **incomplete predication**.

1. When the predicate is completed by the object of the action, the verb is called transitive; as, War brings *sorrow*.

2. When the predicate is completed by an adjunct describing the subject, the verb is intransitive (or in the passive voice), and the completing adjunct is called a complement; as, The sky is *blue;* The boy was called *John.*

An intransitive verb of incomplete predication is sometimes called a **copula,** since it connects or couples the subject with a word describing the subject; as, —

Washington *was* a patriot. She *looks* happy.

A transitive verb of incomplete predication is said to be **factitive** when it takes a complement which describes the direct object of the verb; as, —

They **made** him *captain.* We **set** the prisoner *free.*

The grammatical predicate with its adjuncts is called the **logical,** or **complete, predicate;** as, —

We *are the prisoners of the night.*

ELEMENTS OF A SENTENCE.

The elements of a sentence are **words, phrases, or clauses.**

A **phrase** is a combination of words performing a distinct office in a sentence, but not having a subject and a predicate; as, —

Birds *in the thicket* sing.

Phrases may be named according to their **form:** —

1. A phrase introduced by a preposition is called a **preposi-tional phrase;** as,

The key *to pleasure* is honest work.

2. A phrase introduced by an infinitive is called **an infinitive phrase;** as, —

The sun begins *to gild the morning sky.*

3. A phrase introduced by a participle is called a **participial phrase**; as, —

The pillars *supporting the roof* are strong.

4. A phrase made up of an appositive noun and its modifiers is called an **appositive phrase**; as, —

He comes, *the herald of a noisy world.*

Phrases may be named according to the **office** performed by each : —

1. A phrase that performs the office of an adjective is called an **adjective phrase**; as, —

We heard the roar *of the ocean.*

2. A phrase that performs the office of an adverb is called an **adverbial phrase**; as, —

Once more he stept *into the street.*

3. A phrase that performs the office of a noun is called a **substantive phrase**; as, —

To climb steep hills requires slow pace at first.

A **clause** is a combination of words performing a distinct office in a sentence, and having a subject and a predicate; as, —

Uneasy lies the head *that wears a crown.*

1. A clause that expresses the leading, or principal, thought of a sentence is called an **independent** or **principal clause**; as, —

They trimmed the lamps as the sun went down.

2. A clause that depends upon some other part of the sentence for its full meaning is called a **dependent**, or **subordinate**, **clause**; as, —

They trimmed the lamps *as the sun went down.*

PRINCIPAL ELEMENTS.

The grammatical subject and the grammatical predicate are the **principal elements** of a sentence; as, —

The *shadows dance* upon the wall.

SUBORDINATE ELEMENTS.

The modifiers of the principal elements in a sentence are called **subordinate elements**; as, —

The light *of smiles* shall fill *again*
The lids *that overflow with tears.*

When the predicate verb is of incomplete predication, the object or the complement may be called a modifier of the grammatical predicate; as, —

1. The sexton rang *the bell.*
2. My mirror is *the mountain spring.*

STRUCTURE OF SENTENCES.

Sentences may be **simple, complex,** or **compound.**

A sentence that expresses one thought is called a **simple sentence**; as, —

The march of the human mind is slow,

A sentence consisting of one principal clause and one or more subordinate clauses is called a **complex sentence**; as, —

Some murmur when their sky is clear.

A sentence made up of two or more independent members is called a **compound sentence**; as, —

I listened, but I could not hear.

EXERCISE I.

1. State the difference between the grammatical subject and the logical subject, and give examples of each. 2. State the difference between the principal elements and the subordinate elements of a sentence. Give examples

EXERCISE II.

1. Write three sentences containing adjective phrases.
2. Write three sentences containing adverbial phrases.
3. Write three sentences containing substantive phrases.

LESSON LIX.

THE SIMPLE SENTENCE.

A simple sentence is a sentence that expresses one thought.

THE SUBJECT.

The **subject** of a simple sentence may be —

I. A **noun**; as, —

Birds have many enemies.

II. A **pronoun**; as, —

We expected a different answer.

III. An **infinitive,** or an **infinitive phrase**; as, —

1. *To delay* is dangerous.
2. *To say nothing* is often better than to speak.
3. *Saying nothing* is often better than speaking.

Modifiers of the Subject.

The **subject may be modified by** —

I. An **adjective**; as, —

Still waters run deep.

II. A **noun** or a **pronoun** in the **possessive case**; as, —

1. *Edward's* friends were present.

2. *My* opinion is not changed.

III. An **appositive word** or **phrase.**

1. I, *Paul*, have written it with mine own hand.

2. Hope, *the balm of life*, soothes us under every misfortune.

IV. A **prepositional phrase**, as adjective; as, —

The paths *of glory* lead but to the grave.

V. A **participle**, or a **participial phrase**; as, —

1. *Having sung*, she left the room.

2. *Advancing cautiously*, he opened the door.

VI. An **infinitive**; as, —

His desire *to learn* is great.

The Predicate.

The **predicate** of a simple sentence may be —

I. A complete **verb** —

1. In a **simple form**; as, The sun *rose.*

2. In a **compound form**; as, The sun *has risen.*

II. An incomplete **intransitive verb** completed by —

1. A **noun**; as, He **was** *secretary.*

2. A **pronoun**; as, It **was** *he.*

3. An **adjective**; as, Iron is *hard.*

4. An **infinitive**, or an **infinitive phrase**; as, To see her is *to love her.*

5. An **adverb**, or an **adverbial phrase**; as, The moon is *up;* All the household **are** *at rest.*

III. An incomplete **transitive verb** with its **object** —

1. A **noun**; as, I hear *music.*

2. A **pronoun**; as, We **saw** *them.*

3. An **infinitive**, or an **infinitive phrase**; as, She **likes** *to read.*

4. Or **objects**; as, He **gave** *John* a *book.*

5. And **objective complement**; as, They **made** him *treasurer;* The heat **turned** the milk *sour.*

MODIFIERS OF THE PREDICATE.

The **predicate verb** may be **modified** by —

I. An **adverb**; as, —

The bells ring *merrily.*

II. A **prepositional phrase**, as adverb; as, —

He went *towards the river.*

III. An **infinitive**, or an **infinitive phrase**; as, —

They came *to see the paintings.*

IV. An **adverbial objective**; as, —

She remained two *hours.*

V. A **nominative absolute phrase**; as, —

The war being ended, the soldiers returned.

The phrase, "the war being ended," gives a reason for the return of the soldiers. It is an adverbial phrase, being nearly equivalent in meaning to the adverbial clause, "as the war was ended."

When the subject, the object, or the complement consists of two or more connected terms, it is said to be **compound**; as, —

> *Games* and *carols* closed the busy day.
> Learn *to labor* and *to wait*.
> Her voice was *low* and *sweet*.

Modifiers may be **simple, compound,** or **complex** —
A modifier consisting of a single word or phrase is **simple.**

> The ship went *slowly*.
> We spoke not a word *of sorrow*.

A modifier consisting of two or more connected words or phrases is **compound**; as, —

> The ship went *slowly and smoothly*.
> His cohorts were gleaming *in purple and gold*.

A modifier consisting of a word or phrase with modifiers of its own is **complex**; as, —

> The ship went *very slowly*.
> Here rests his head *upon the lap of earth*.

A **series of adjectives** may form a compound or a complex modifier; as, —

> 1. He was an *honest, temperate, forgiving* man.
> 2. *Two large elm* trees stood near the house.

In the first example the adjectives are co-ordinate, each modifying the same noun. Adjectives used in this manner may be separated by commas or joined by conjunctions.

In the second example the adjectives form a complex modifier. Thus —

Two modifies the whole expression *large elm trees.*
Large modifies *elm trees.*
Elm modifies *trees.*

EXERCISE I.

Write sentences in which the subject is —

1. A noun modified by an adjective.
2. A noun modified by a possessive pronoun.
3. A noun modified by an appositive phrase.
4. A noun modified by a prepositional phrase.
5. A pronoun modified by a participial phrase.
6. An infinitive phrase.

EXERCISE II.

Write sentences in which the predicate is —

1. A complete verb modified by an adverb.
2. A complete verb modified by a prepositional phrase.
3. A complete verb modified by an infinitive phrase.
4. A complete verb modified by an adverbial objective.
5. An intransitive verb completed by a noun.
6. An intransitive verb completed by a pronoun.
7. An intransitive verb completed by an adjective.
8. An intransitive verb completed by an infinitive.
9. A transitive verb with an infinitive as a direct object.
10. A transitive verb with a direct and an indirect object.
11. A transitive verb with a direct object and an objective complement.

LESSON LX.

ANALYSIS OF SIMPLE SENTENCES.

Analyze orally the following sentences, thus: —

1. Tell the kind of sentence.
2. Name the subject and the predicate.
3. Tell what the subject consists of.
4. Tell what the predicate consists of.

Example I.— *This old ship had been laden with immense wealth.*

ORAL ANALYSIS.

1. This is a simple declarative sentence.

2. The subject is *this old ship;* the predicate, *had been laden with immense wealth.*

3. The subject consists of the noun *ship*, with the adjectives *this* and *old*, of which *old* modifies *ship*, and *this* modifies *old ship.*

4. The predicate consists of the verb *had been laden*, modified by the adverbial phrase *with immense wealth.*

Or,

Write the analysis briefly as follows: —

WRITTEN ANALYSIS.

Simple Declarative Sentence.

I. — SUBJECT.

Subject . . . . This old ship.
Subject noun . . . . ship.

Modifiers of subject noun . . . . $\begin{cases} \text{this.} & (\textit{Adjective.}) \\ \text{old.} & (\textit{Adjective.}) \end{cases}$

II. — PREDICATE.

Predicate . . . . had been laden with immense wealth.
Predicate verb . . . . had been laden.
Modifier of predicate verb . . . . with immense wealth. (*Adverbial phrase.*)

Example II.— *The prospect of success seemed small.*

ORAL ANALYSIS.

1. This is a simple declarative sentence.

2. The subject is *the prospect of success;* the predicate, *seemed small.*

3. The subject consists of the noun *prospect,* modified by the adjective *the* and by the adjective phrase *of success.*

4. The predicate consists of the verb *seemed,* completed by the adjective *small.*

WRITTEN ANALYSIS.

Simple Declarative Sentence.

I. — SUBJECT.

Subject . . . . The prospect of success.
Subject noun . . . . prospect.
Modifiers of subject noun . . . . $\begin{cases} \text{the.} & (\textit{Adjective.}) \\ \text{of success.} & (\textit{Adjective phrase.}) \end{cases}$

II. — PREDICATE.

Predicate . . . . seemed small.
Predicate verb . . . . seemed.
Complement . . . . small. (*Adjective.*)

Example III. — *Having obtained the desired information, he left the room.*

ORAL ANALYSIS.

1. This is a simple declarative sentence.

2. The subject is *he having obtained the desired information;* the predicate, *left the room.*

3. The subject consists of the pronoun *he,* modified by the participial phrase, *having obtained the desired information.*

4. The predicate consists of the verb *left,* completed by the object *room,* which is modified by *the.*

WRITTEN ANALYSIS.

Simple Declarative Sentence.

I. — SUBJECT.

Subject . . . . he having obtained the desired information.
Subject pronoun . . . . he.
Modifier of subject pronoun . . . Having obtained the desired information.   (*Participial phrase.*)

II. — PREDICATE.

Predicate . . . . left the room.
Predicate verb . . . . left.
Object . . . . room   (*Noun.*)
Modifier of object . . . . the. (*Adjective.*)

Example IV. — *It is useless to deny the fact.*

ORAL ANALYSIS.

1. This is a simple declarative sentence.

2. The grammatical subject is *it,* which stands for the logical subject, *to deny the fact;* the predicate, *is useless.*

3. The logical subject is the infinitive phrase, *to deny the fact*, placed after the verb.

4. The predicate consists of the verb *is*, completed by the adjective *useless*.

WRITTEN ANALYSIS.

Simple Declarative Sentence.

I. — SUBJECT.

Logical subject . . . . To deny the fact. (*Infinitive phrase.*)
Grammatical subject . . . . It.

II. — PREDICATE.

Predicate . . . . is useless.
Predicate verb . . . . is.
Complement . . . . useless. (*Adjective.*)

SENTENCES FOR ANALYSIS.

EXERCISE I.

1. The decision of the judge increased the irritation of the people.

2. The best honey is the product of the milder parts of the temperate zone. — JOHN BURROUGHS.

3. The captain's share of the treasure was enough to make him comfortable for the rest of his days. — HAWTHORNE.

4. I stand upon my native hills again. — BRYANT.

5. Every man is a missionary for good or for evil.

6. We are equally served by receiving and by imparting.

7. A low, white-washed room, with a stone floor, carefully scrubbed, served for parlor, kitchen, and hall. — IRVING

8. My friend, Sir Roger, being a good churchman, has beautified the inside of his church with several texts of his own choosing. — ADDISON.

9. It is the glory of a man to pass by an offence.

10. The great secret of a good style is to have proper words in proper places. — E. P. WHIPPLE.

EXERCISE II.

1. Thinking it would be cold in the cave, we had brought warm wraps.

2. How strangely the past is peeping over the shoulders of the present!

3. The words of mercy were upon his lips.

4. Chimney swallows have almost abandoned hollow trees for their nesting-places, even in our most thickly wooded areas, preferring our chimneys.

5. Early next morning I went to visit the grounds.

6. Having been accustomed to the control of large bodies of men, I had not much difficulty in comprehending the situation.

7. Hundreds of other carriages, crowded with their thousands of men, were hastening to the great city.

8. The Stamp Act was a direct tax laid upon the whole American people by Parliament. — JOHN FISKE.

9. I see everywhere the gardens, the vineyards, the orchards, with the various greens of the olive, the fig, and the orange. — C. D. WARNER.

10. A truly great man borrows no lustre from splendid ancestry.

11. Success being hopeless, preparations were made for a retreat.

12. To bear is to conquer our fate. — CAMPBELL.

LESSON LXI.

THE COMPLEX SENTENCE.

A *complex sentence* is a sentence consisting of one principal clause and of one or more subordinate clauses; as, —

He who would search for pearls must dive below.

The principal clause expresses the leading or principal thought of a sentence, but it does not express the complete thought.

The subordinate clause performs the office of a noun, an adjective, or an adverb, and is usually introduced by a conjunction or by a relative pronoun.

I. — SUBSTANTIVE CLAUSES.

A clause that performs the office of a noun is called a **noun clause** or a **substantive clause**.

A substantive clause may be used —

1. As the **subject of a verb**; as, —

That you have wronged me doth appear in this.

2. As a **predicate nominative**; as, —

The result was *that the treaty was signed.*

3. As the **object of a transitive verb**; as, —

He knows *who wrote the letter.*

4. As the **logical subject**, defining a foregoing introductory, or grammatical subject; as, —

It was a fortunate thing *that we met him.*

5. As the **object of a preposition**; as, —

The leader encouraged his men by *what he said* and by *what he did.*

Substantive clauses are introduced by the conjunction *that*, and by the words *how, when, who, what,* etc.

The conjunction *that* is often omitted when the noun clause follows the principal verb; as, —

I hope [*that*] he will succeed.

II. — ADJECTIVE CLAUSES.

•A clause that performs the office of an adjective is called an **adjective clause**; as, —

Sweet are the thoughts *that savor of content.*

I remember, I remember

The house *where I was born.*

Adjective clauses are introduced by the relative pronouns *who, which, that, what,* and by the adverbs *when, where, whence,* etc.

III. — ADVERBIAL CLAUSES.

A clause that performs the office of an adverb is called an **adverbial clause**.

An adverbial clause may denote —

1. **Time**, introduced by *after, before, since, till, when, while;* as, —

Let us live *while we live.*

2. **Place**, introduced by *where, whence, whither;* as, —

I shall remain *where I am.*

3. **Manner,** introduced by *as; as,* —

    The days of man are but *as grass* [*is*].

4. **Degree,** introduced by *than, as;* as, —

    My days are swifter *than a weaver's shuttle* [*is swift*].
    Enough is as good *as a feast* [*is good*].

5. **Cause or Reason,** introduced by *because, for, since, as, that;* as, —

    Freely we serve, *because we freely love.*
    Since you desire it, I will remain.

6. **Purpose,** introduced by *that, lest;* as, —

    Open the door *that they may enter.*
    Take heed *lest ye fall.*

7. **Condition,** introduced by *if, unless, except, but;* as, —

    I will go *if you are ready.*
    The house will be sold *unless the money is paid.*
    Except ye repent, ye shall all likewise perish.
    It never rains *but it pours.*

8. **Concession,** introduced by *though, although;* as, —

    Though he works hard, he does not succeed.
    Although he spoke, he said nothing.

EXERCISE I.—SUBSTANTIVE CLAUSES.

Mention the substantive clauses in the following sentences, and tell how each is used: —

1. We can prove that the earth is round.
2. What he said was not understood.

3. That the work is well done is not to be denied.

4. The consequence was that the army gained a victory.

5. It is generally admitted that they acted with energy and foresight.

6. He did not know what the message meant.

7. The fact that he was absent is significant.

8. But that I am forbid, I could a tale unfold.

EXERCISE II.—ADJECTIVE CLAUSES.

Point out the adjective clauses in the following sentences, and tell what each modifies: —

1. He that is giddy thinks the world turns round.

2. In the evening we reached a village where I had determined to pass the night.

3. It was the time when lilies blow.

4. The evil that men do lives after them.

5. I had a dream which was not all a dream.

6. He serves all who dares be true.

7. Nature never did betray the heart that loved her.

8. One by one we miss the voices which we loved so well to hear.

EXERCISE III.—ADVERBIAL CLAUSES.

Mention the adverbial clauses in the following sentences, and state what each denotes: —

1. My punishment is greater than I can bear.

2. Make hay while the sun shines.

3. Since my country calls me, I obey.

4. He sleeps wherever night overtakes him.

5. Forgive us our debts, as we forgive our debtors.

6. Love not sleep, lest thou come to poverty.

7. He flourisheth as a flower of the field.

8. Whither thou goest, I will go.

9.   Not as the conqueror comes
        They, the true-hearted, came.

10. It droppeth as the gentle rain from heaven.

11. Though I be rude in speech, yet not in knowledge.

12. Your people are as cheerless as your clime [is cheerless].

LESSON LXII.

ANALYSIS OF COMPLEX SENTENCES.

To analyze a complex sentence —

1. Tell the kind of sentence.
2. Name the subject and the predicate of the sentence.
3. Tell what the subject consists of.
4. Tell what the predicate consists of.
5. Analyze the subordinate clause or clauses.

Example 1.—*That man is formed for social life is acknowledged by all.*

ORAL ANALYSIS.

1. This is a complex declarative sentence.

2. The subject is the noun clause, *that man is formed for social life ;* the predicate, *is acknowledged by all.*

3. The predicate consists of the verb *is acknowledged,* modified by the adverbial phrase *by all.*

4. The subordinate clause is introduced by the conjunction *that*.

5. The subject of the subordinate clause is the noun *man ;* the predicate, *is formed for social life.*

6. The predicate of the clause consists of the verb *is formed*, modified by the adverbial phrase *for social life.*

WRITTEN ANALYSIS.

Complex Declarative Sentence.

I. — SUBJECT.

Subject . . . . That man is formed for social life. (*Noun clause.*)

II. — PREDICATE.

Predicate . . . . is acknowledged by all.
Predicate verb . . . . is acknowledged.
Modifier of predicate verb . . . by all. (*Adverbial phrase.*)

Subordinate Clause.

Introduced by the conjunction *that.*

I. — SUBJECT.

Subject . . . . man.

II. — PREDICATE.

Predicate . . . . is formed for social life.
Predicate verb . . . . is formed.
Modifier of predicate verb . . . for social life. (*Adverbial phrase.*)

Example II. — *The fact that he was present is sufficient.*

ORAL ANALYSIS.

1. This is a complex declarative sentence.

2. The subject is *the fact that he was present ;* the predicate, *is sufficient.*

3. The subject consists of the noun *fact*, modified by the adjective *the*, and by the appositive noun clause *that he was present.*

4. The predicate consists of the verb *is*, completed by the adjective *sufficient.*

5. The subordinate clause is connected to the noun *fact* by the conjunction *that.*

6. The subject of the subordinate clause is *he;* the predicate, *was present.*

7. The predicate of the clause consists of the verb *was*, completed by the adjective *present.*

WRITTEN ANALYSIS.

Complex Declarative Sentence.

I. — SUBJECT.

Subject.	The fact that he was present.
Subject noun	fact.
Modifiers of subject noun	{ the. (*Adjective.*) { that he was present. (*Appositive clause*)

II. — PREDICATE.

Predicate	is sufficient.
Predicate verb	is.
Complement	sufficient. (*Adjective.*)

Subordinate Clause.

Connected to the noun *fact* by the conjunction *that.*

I. — SUBJECT.

Subject.	he.

II. — PREDICATE.

Predicate	was present.
Predicate verb	was.
Complement	present. (*Adjective.*)

Example III. — *The people believed in him, because he was honest and true.*

WRITTEN ANALYSIS.

Complex Declarative Sentence.

I. — SUBJECT.

Subject . . . . The people.
Subject noun . . . . people.
Modifier of subject noun . the. (*Adjective.*)

II. — PREDICATE.

Predicate . . . . believed in him, because he was honest and true.
Predicate verb . . . . believed.
Modifiers of predicate verb . . . { in him. (*Adverbial phrase.*)
because he was honest and true. (*Adverbial clause of Reason.*)

Subordinate Clause.

Connected to the verb *believed*, by the conjunction *because*, expressing *Reason*.

I. — SUBJECT.

Subject . . . . he.

II. — PREDICATE.

Predicate . . . . was honest and true.
Predicate verb . . . . was.
Complement of predicate . . . . honest and true. (*Adjectives* connected by *and.*)

Example IV. — *Beware lest you fall.*

WRITTEN ANALYSIS.

Complex Imperative Sentence.

I. — SUBJECT.

Subject . . . . [you] *understood.*

II. — PREDICATE.

Predicate . . . . Beware lest you fall

Predicate verb . . . . Beware.

Modifier of predicate verb . . . lest you fall. (*Adverbial clause of Purpose*)

Subordinate Clause.

Connected to verb *beware*, by the conjunction *lest*, expressing *Purpose*.

Subject. . . . . you.

Predicate . . . . fall.

Analyze the sentences in the following exercises: —

EXERCISE L

1. As we approached the house, we heard the sound of music.

2. Such a fortnight in the woods as I have been lightly sketching, will bring to him who rightly uses it a rich return.

3. If we seek to acquire the style of another, we renounce the individual style which we might have acquired.

4. "Good speed!" cried the watch, as the gate-bolts undrew.

5. So thick were the fluttering snow-flakes, that even the trees were hidden by them the greater part of the time.

6. I now found myself among noble avenues of oaks and elms, whose vast size bespoke the growth of centuries.

7. Nothing is so dangerous as pride.

8. We are happy now because God wills it. — LOWELL.

9. A great black cloud had been gathering in the sky for some time past, although it had not yet overspread the sun.

10. Here I sit among my descendants, in my old armchair, and immemorial corner, while the firelight throws an appropriate glory round my venerable frame. — HAWTHORNE.

11. He who sets a great example is great. — VICTOR HUGO.

12. I saw from the beach, when the morning was shining,
A bark o'er the waters move gloriously on. — MOORE.

EXERCISE II.

1. The song that moves a Nation's heart
Is in itself a deed. — TENNYSON.

2. As I crossed the bridge over the Avon on my return, I paused to contemplate the distant church in which the poet lies buried. — IRVING.

3. We hold these truths to be self-evident: that all men are created equal; that they are endowed by their Creator with certain unalienable rights; that among these are life, liberty, and the pursuit of happiness.

4. We can almost fancy that we are visiting him [Milton] in his small lodging; that we see him sitting at the old organ beneath the faded green hangings; that we can catch the quick twinkle of his eyes, rolling in vain to find the day; that we are reading in the lines of his noble countenance the proud and mournful history of his glory and his affliction. — MACAULAY.

5. When the woodpecker is searching for food, or laying siege to some hidden grub, the sound of his hammer is dead or muffled, and is heard but a few yards. It is only upon dry, seasoned timber, freed of its bark, that he beats his reveille to spring and woos his mate. — JOHN BURROUGHS.

LESSON LXIII.

THE COMPOUND SENTENCE.

A compound sentence is a sentence made up of two or more independent members; as, —

The walls are high, and the shores are steep.

Each member of a compound sentence, by itself, forms a complete sentence, which may be simple or complex; as, —

The Mayor was dumb, and *the Council stood*
As if they were changed into blocks of wood.

1. The Mayor was dumb. (Simple Sentence.)
2. The Council stood as if they were changed into blocks of wood. (Complex Sentence.)

The connective between the members may be omitted, but the relation between the members should be stated in the analysis; as, —

The night is chill, the cloud is gray.

To analyze a compound sentence —

1. Tell the kind of sentence.
2 Name the different members, and tell how they are connected.
3. Analyze in order the different members of the sentence.

Example. — *The merchants shut up their warehouses, and the laboring men stood idle about the wharves.*

ORAL ANALYSIS.

1. This is a compound declarative sentence, consisting of two simple members connected by the copulative conjunction, *and.*
2. The subject of the first member is *the merchants;* the predi-

cate, *shut up their warehouses.* The subject consists of the noun *merchants*, modified by the adjective *the.* The predicate consists of the verb *shut*, modified by the adverb *up*, and completed by the object *warehouses.* The object is modified by the possessive pronoun *their.*

3. The subject of the second member is *the laboring men;* the predicate, *stood idle about the wharves.* The subject consists of the noun *men*, modified by the phrase *the laboring*, of which *laboring* modifies *men*, and *the* modifies *laboring men.* The predicate consists of the verb *stood*, completed by the adjective *idle*, and modified by the adverbial phrase *about the wharves.*

WRITTEN ANALYSIS.

Compound Declarative Sentence.

Two members connected by the conjunction *and.*

FIRST MEMBER.

I. — SUBJECT.

Subject	The merchants.
Subject noun	merchants.
Modifier of subject noun	the. (*Adjective.*)

II. — PREDICATE.

Predicate	shut up their warehouses.
Predicate verb	shut.
Modifier of predicate verb . . .	up. (*Adverb.*)
Object	warehouses.
Modifier of object	their. (*Possessive pronoun.*)

SECOND MEMBER.

I. — SUBJECT.

Subject	the laboring men.
Subject noun	men.
Modifiers of subject noun	{ laboring. (*Adjective.*) { the. (*Adjective.*)

II. — PREDICATE.

Predicate . . . . stood idle about the wharves.
Predicate verb . . . . stood.
Complement . . . . idle. .
Modifier of predicate verb . . . about the wharves. (*Adverbial phrase*)

Analyze the sentences in the following exercises: —

EXERCISE I.

1. Every day is a little life; and our whole life is but a day repeated.

2. The harvest truly is plenteous, but the laborers are few.

3. They toil not, neither do they spin.

4. It is one thing to be well informed; it is another to be wise.

5. The ravine was full of sand now, but it had once been full of water.

6. He touched his harp, and nations heard, entranced.

7. The moon is up, and yet it is not night. — BYRON.

8.　　Stay, rivulet, nor haste to leave
　　　　The lovely vale that lies around thee. — BRYANT.

9. They had played together in infancy; they had worked together in manhood; they were now tottering about, and gossiping away the evening of life; and in a short time they will probably be buried together in the neighboring churchyard. — IRVING.

10. Now stir the fire, and close the shutters fast. — COWPER.

EXERCISE II.

1.　　Lay down the axe; fling by the spade;
　　　　Leave in its track the toiling plough. — BRYANT.

2. I turned in my saddle and made its girths tight.

3. He assisted at their sports, made their playthings, taught them to fly kites and shoot marbles, and told them long stories of ghosts, witches, and Indians. — IRVING.

4.
        That was the grandest funeral
        That ever passed on earth;
        Yet no man heard the trampling,
        Or saw the train go forth.

5. But what chiefly characterized the colonists of Merry Mount was their veneration for the Maypole. It has made their true history a poet's tale. Spring decked the hallowed emblem with young blossoms and fresh green boughs; Summer brought roses of the deepest blush, and the perfected foliage of the forest; Autumn enriched it with that red and yellow gorgeousness which converts each wildwood leaf into a painted flower; and Winter silvered it with sleet, and hung it round with icicles, till it flashed in the cold sunshine, itself a frozen sunbeam. — HAWTHORNE.

LESSON LXIV.

SELECTIONS FOR ANALYSIS.

I.

THE ARROW AND THE SONG.

I shot an arrow into the air,
It fell to earth, I knew not where;
For, so swiftly it flew, the sight
Could not follow it in its flight.

I breathed a song into the air,
It fell to earth, I knew not where;
For who has sight so keen and strong
That it can follow the flight of song?

Long, long afterward, in an oak
I found the arrow, still unbroke;
And the song, from beginning to end,
I found again in the heart of a friend.
— HENRY WADSWORTH LONGFELLOW.

II.

RIP VAN WINKLE.

The great error in Rip's composition was an insuperable aversion to all kinds of profitable labor. It could not be from the want of assiduity or perseverance; for he would sit on a wet rock, with a rod as long and heavy as a Tartar's lance, and fish all day without a murmur, even though he should not be encouraged by a single nibble. He would carry a fowling-piece on his shoulder for hours together, trudging through woods and swamps, and up hill and down dale, to shoot a few squirrels or wild pigeons. He would never refuse to assist a neighbor, even in the roughest toil, and was a foremost man at all country frolics for husking Indian corn or building stone fences. The women of the village, too, used to employ him to run their errands, and to do such little odd jobs as their less obliging husbands would not do for them; — in a word, Rip was ready to attend to anybody's business but his own; but as to doing family duty, and keeping his farm in order, he found it impossible.

In fact, he declared it was of no use to work on his farm; it was the most pestilent little piece of ground in the whole country; everything about it went wrong, and would go wrong in spite of him. His fences were continually falling to pieces; his cow would either go astray, or get among the cabbages; weeds were sure to grow quicker in his fields than anywhere else; the rain always made a point of setting in just as he had some out-door work to do; so that though his patrimonial estate had dwindled away under his management, acre by acre, until there was little more left than a mere patch of Indian corn and potatoes, yet it was the worst-conditioned farm in the neighborhood.

—WASHINGTON IRVING.

III.

THE POET'S SONG.

The rain had fallen, the Poet arose,
　　He passed by the town and out of the street,
A light wind blew from the gates of the sun,
　　And waves of shadow went over the wheat,
And he sat him down in a lonely place,
　　And chanted a melody loud and sweet,
That made the wild-swan pause in her cloud,
　　And the lark drop down at his feet.

The swallow stopt as he hunted the bee,
　　The snake slipt under a spray,
The wild hawk stood with the down on his beak,

And stared, with his foot on the prey,
And the nightingale thought, " I have sung many songs,
But never a one so gay,
For he sings of what the world will be
When the years have died away." —ALFRED TENNYSON

IV.

LEAVES.

The leaves, as we shall see immediately, are the feeders of the plant. Their own orderly habits of succession must not interfere with their main business of finding food. Where the sun and air are, the leaf must go, whether it be out of order or not. So, therefore, in any group, the first consideration with the young leaves is much like that of young bees, how to keep out of each other's way, that every one may at once leave its neighbors as much free-air pasture as possible, and obtain a relative freedom for itself. This would be a quite simple matter, and produce other simply balanced forms, if each branch, with open air all round it, had nothing to think of but reconcilement of interests among its own leaves. But every branch has others to meet or to cross, sharing with them, in various advantage, what shade, or sun, or rain is to be had. Hence every single leaf-cluster presents the general aspect of a little family, entirely at unity among themselves, but obliged to get their living by various shifts, concessions, and infringements of the family rules, in order not to invade the privileges of other people in their neighborhood.

—JOHN RUSKIN,

INDEX.

———◦∘◦———

BIBLIOLIFE

Old Books Deserve a New Life
www.bibliolife.com

Did you know that you can get most of our titles in our trademark **EasyScript**[TM] print format? **EasyScript**[TM] provides readers with a larger than average typeface, for a reading experience that's easier on the eyes.

Did you know that we have an ever-growing collection of books in many languages?

Order online:
www.bibliolife.com/store

Or to exclusively browse our **EasyScript**[TM] collection:
www.bibliogrande.com

At BiblioLife, we aim to make knowledge more accessible by making thousands of titles available to you – quickly and affordably.

Contact us:
BiblioLife
PO Box 21206
Charleston, SC 29413